Edward Bulwer Lytton

Bulwer's Lady of Lyons

With a Complete Idiomatical and Grammatical Vocabulary for....

Edward Bulwer Lytton

Bulwer's Lady of Lyons
With a Complete Idiomatical and Grammatical Vocabulary for....

ISBN/EAN: 9783337125318

Printed in Europe, USA, Canada, Australia, Japan

Cover: Foto ©Thomas Meinert / pixelio.de

More available books at **www.hansebooks.com**

BULWER'S
LADY OF LYONS

WITH A COMPLETE

IDIOMATICAL AND GRAMMATICAL VOCABULARY

FOR

TRANSLATION FROM ENGLISH INTO FRENCH

PRECEDED BY A SYNOPSIS OF THE MOST USEFUL RULES OF FRENCH
GRAMMAR, AND A METHODICAL TABLE OF ALL IRREG-
ULAR VERBS OCCURRING IN THE TEXT.

ALSO, VARIOUS SUBJECTS FOR

ORIGINAL COMPOSITION IN FRENCH,

MOST OF THEM UNDER THE FORM (ADOPTED AT OXFORD AND AT WEST POINT)
OF SHORT LETTERS IN FRENCH, TO BE ANSWERED
IN THE SAME LANGUAGE.

By B. MAURICE, A. M.

*Professor in the Baltimore Female College; Late Assistant
Professor U. S. Naval Academy.*

NEW YORK
HENRY HOLT AND COMPANY
F. W. CHRISTERN
BOSTON: CARL SCHOENHOF

58286

PREFACE.

In adopting the text of Bulwer's "Lady of Lyons" for the purpose of translation from English into French, we have been influenced by the following reasons, among others:

1. It is a PLAY. The translation of dialogue will teach French polite conversation better than any other exercise could do.

2. The text embraces almost every variety of style, from ordinary every-day discourse to the most sublime and poetical descriptions.

3. The scene of the play is *in France, and in modern times;* which peculiarly fits it for our purpose.

4. After being translated by classes, the play may be represented on the stage, in French, *by its own translators,* or the students may be required to translate it again, "*à livre ouvert,*" from the English text alone.

To render the book more practical, we have divided the play into sections of from ten to fourteen lines, each complete in sense, so that any section may be given *at random* to the students. And to make it *progressive,* in the first act we have given all needful help to the student by copious references, reducing the number in the three middle acts, and dispensing with them entirely in the last act.

We consider our Vocabulary one of the best features of the work, serving as it does the double purpose of a lexicon and of explanatory foot-notes. The true place for the settlement of idiomatic difficulties is in a vocabulary; the student is then enabled to judge of the *ensemble* of each word, without the loss of time which would be incurred in consulting a number of detached notes.

When idiomatic expressions occur in the text, a star (*) is placed after the *leading word,* which means, "See this word in the Vocabulary, and read there all that pertains to it."

(3)

Again, if there is a rule of grammar concerning a single word (as, for instance, the rule concerning the pluralizing of *vingt* and *cent*), we give the rule in the Vocabulary with the word in question.

A few minor improvements may be here specified.

Words that are *alike* in both languages are not given in the Vocabulary. But, to save the student the trouble of searching for a word which he will not find, we indicate, in the text of the play, all words that are *alike* in both languages, together with their *gender.*

Words beginning with *h* mute are marked, as well as the verbs of the first conjugation whose accidence is in any way peculiar.

We indicate also when a verb is irregular. This feature, coupled with the list of irregular verbs, will prove of great service to the student.

When a word has several meanings entirely different, we give (by means of a synonym between parentheses) a clue for the student to make his choice.

In giving the general rules of the French syntax, necessary for the translation of the " Lady of Lyons," our aim is to make our text-book independent, so that it may be used with any grammar, or even without a grammar, provided the pupils are already well acquainted with the ordinary rules of accidence.

During the early part of their studies, learners have to undergo a patient and slow process of *analysis,* which is done by learning the rules one by one, with corresponding exercises. But when they have attained a certain degree of proficiency they ought to be required to condense what they have learned, to make a kind of philosophical synthesis out of their acquired knowledge.

It is to help them in this work that we have given them, in a few pages, all the general rules of syntax necessary for the correct translation of our text-book.

We have also thought it advisable to give a few subjects for original compositions in French, as the natural terminus of French studies. As to the form of these subjects (which is not ours), we are sure that our colleagues will not fail to appreciate the feature of short letters in French to be answered in the same language.

B. MAURICE.

January 1, 1873.

CONTENTS.

1*

PART FIRST.

SYNTHESIS OF GRAMMATICAL RULES

IRREGULAR VERBS.

(7)

SELECT RULES

Of the most frequent recurrence; the mastering of which is especially recommended for correct writing in French, either by way of TRANSLATION *or* ORIGINAL COMPOSITION.

I. EUPHONY.

Euphony plays a prominent part in many a rule of the French syntax, and forms the chief basis of the rules concerning: 1. the *Elision;* 2. the *Contraction;* 3. the *Verbs of the First Conjugation;* 4. the *Euphonic Letters* -*t*- and *l'*.

§ 1. **Elision** consists in dropping the final vowel of certain words (about a *dozen*, mostly *monosyllables* ending in *e mute*) and replacing that vowel by an apostrophe before words commencing with a *vowel* or an *h mute*.[1]

JE, ME, TE, SE, LE, DE, NE, QUE are subject to elision.

LA, article and pronoun feminine, is the only word in *a* subject to it.

SI (if) is elided only before the masculine pronouns, *il, ils:* as, *s'il vient, s'ils arrivent.*

§ 2. CE, pronoun demonstrative, being subject to the verb *être*, is elided only in the following forms: *c'est, c'était, c'étaient, c'eut été, c'en est fait.*

CE, adjective demonstrative masculine, is not subject to

---

[1] In the Vocabulary, words commencing with an *h mute* are marked by an apostrophe, as *'homme, 'héroïne:* those not marked are aspirate, and no elision takes place with them.

A*

elision, but becomes *cet* before a vowel or an *h* mute : *cet enfant, cet homme, cet excellent citoyen.*

§ 3. MA, TA, SA, feminine forms of the possessive adjective, are not subject to elision, but, for the same reason of euphony, assume the masculine forms *mon, ton, son,* before a vowel or an *h* mute : *mon âme, son humeur, ton excellente mère.* (*Ame, humeur,* and *mère* are feminine nouns.)

GRAND'MÈRE, *grand'tante, grand'messe, entr'acte,* and some few others that practice will teach, are irregular elisions authorized by custom.

§ 4. **Contraction** consists in blending the masculine article *le,* and *les,* plural of both genders, with the preposition *de* or *à,* so as to form a single word out of two : thus, *de le* becomes *du ; de les* becomes *des ; à le* is changed into *au,* and *à les* into *aux.* There is no contraction in the singular when (the following word beginning with a vowel or *h* mute) the elision is to take place : *de l'homme, à l'enfant.*

Remarks on Verbs of the First Conjugation ending in *cer, ger, eyer, ayer, oyer, uyer, eler, eter, emer, ener, ever, eger,* etc.

§ 5. CER : the *c* takes a cedilla before *a* and *o :* as, *nous menaçons, il plaça.*

GER : *e* mute is put after the *g* before *a* and *o :* as, *nous mangeons, ils partageaient.*

§ 6. UYER and OYER change *y* into *i* before *e* mute : as *j'emploie, j'appuie.*

YER generally retains the *y :* as, *je paye.*

§ 7. ELER and ETER double the *l* or *t* before *e* mute : as, *j'appelle, ils jettent.* But the following verbs, instead of doubling *l* or *t,* take the grave accent on the first *e* when the last syllable of their tenses is in *e* mute : *geler, il gèle; acheter, ils achètent,* and a few others.

§ 8. EMER, ENER, ESER, EVER, take the grave accent when the last syllable is mute: *semer, je sème ; se promener, elle se promène ; se lever, ils se lèvent.*

ÉLER, ÉTER, ÉRER, ÉGNER, change the acute into the grave accent before *e* mute : as, *répéter, je répète ; révéler, ils révèlent*; except the future and conditional : *je répéterais, tu persévéreras.*

But ÉGER always retains *é* before *e* mute : as, *protéger, je protège.*

§ 9. **Euphonic letters** -T- and L'. -T- euphonic (with two hyphens) is placed between the verb conjugated interrogatively and its subject *il, elle, on,* when the third person singular of such verb ends in *a* or *e* mute : *a-t-il; aura-t-elle ; parle-t-il ; dira-t-on.*

L' euphonic is sometimes placed before *on* at the beginning of a sentence: *On dit,* or, *L'on dit.* But it must always be used in the middle of a sentence, to prevent the cacophonic encounter of two vowels : *Il faut savoir où* L'ON *nous mène* (OÙ ON *nous mène* would not be euphonic).

II. ARTICLE—ITS USE AND OMISSION.

Use. *As a general rule, whenever we find an article in English, we use the corresponding one in French. The differences of usage are as follows :*

§ 1. The DEFINITE ARTICLE is used in French before all substantives taken in a general sense, although it is omitted in English in such cases :

La paresse est la mère de tous les vices, Idleness is the mother of all the vices.

§ 2. Before names of countries, provinces, winds, rivers,

and mountains : *La France, le Maryland, les Alleghanies.* Also, before adjectives (then always masculine) taken substantively : *Le vert et le bleu; joindre l'utile à l'agréable.*

§ 3. Before titles : *Le général Scott, le Président Thiers.* In respectful address, the French make use of the words *Monsieur, Madame, Mademoiselle,* before titles and designations of relationship : *Monsieur le Maréchal, Madame la Duchesse, Mademoiselle votre sœur.*

§ 4. The English make use of the indefinite article *a* or *an* before nouns of measure, weight, and number ; but the French use the article *le, la : Un franc le mètre; douze sous la livre.* Except in speaking of time, when the indefinite article is expressed by the preposition *par : Deux fois* PAR *semaine; mille francs* PAR *an.*

(For other rules concerning *a* or *an,* see that word in the Vocabulary.)

§ 5. Before nouns taken in a partitive sense (*some* or *any* expressed or understood in English) the French make use of the preposition *de* with the definite article *le, la, les : Du pain, de la viande, des livres.* (See § 9.)

Omission. The French omit the article—

§ 6. Before nouns simply qualifying a preceding noun : *Table de marbre, bouteille de vin, histoire de France.*

§ 7. Before nouns used adjectively or in apposition : *Charles est soldat; Philippe, roi de Macédoine.*

§ 8. After adverbs of quantity : *Beaucoup de bruit, peu d'effet, combien de morts.*

§ 9. In the partitive sense, the definite article is omitted and the preposition *de* alone is used, when the sentence is *negative,* and also when the adjective comes *before* the noun : *Nous n'avons pas d'argent; nous avons entendu d'excellente musique.*

III. AGREEMENT.

Three principal rules of agreement:—§ 1. Of articles, adjectives, and pronouns of all kinds, with their noun ; §§ 2, 3, 4. Of the Past Participle ; § 5. Of verbs with their subject.

§ 1. WHEN about to translate a sentence, the student should carefully ascertain the gender of the noun ; for the *substantive is the leading word.* ARTICLES, ADJECTIVES qualificative and determinative, PRONOUNS of all kinds (demonstrative, possessive, indefinite), agree in *gender* and *number* with the noun they qualify or to which they refer.

Adjectives qualifying two or more nouns in the singular are put in the plural ; and if the nouns are of different genders, the adjective is put in the *plural masculine.*

§ 2. PAST PARTICIPLES conjugated with the auxiliary *être* or *without auxiliary* agree, like adjectives, in gender and number with the word they qualify.

§ 3. If conjugated with the auxiliary *avoir*, they agree with the direct regimen of the verb, if that direct regimen *precedes;* but they remain invariable if the direct regimen follows, or if there is no direct regimen.

Ex. *Les livres bien* IMPRIMÉS *sont toujours* PRÉFÉRÉS *par les élèves. La pomme que j'ai* CUEILLIE, *je l'ai* MANGÉE. *Elle s'est* COUPÉ *le doigt.*

§ 4. *Rem.* Past participles of *reflective verbs*, though always conjugated with *être*, follow the rule of the past participle with *avoir*, namely, they agree with the direct regimen when it *precedes*, and remain unchanged if it follows.

Ex. *Lucrèce s'est* TUÉE ; *elle s'est* DONNÉ *la mort.*

§ 5. A verb agrees with its subject in number and person, as in English ; collective nouns only making a difference in the two syntaxes.

In English, a noun subject in the singular, if it implies collection or plurality, governs its verb either in the singular or in the plural; but in French, all words referring to a noun in the singular are put in that number, though the noun may imply an idea of plurality; like *famille* (family), *Directoire* (the Directory, composed of five members).

Ex.   The jury were in session all night, *le jury siégea toute la nuit;* they were very much divided, IL *était très-divisé.*

IV. GOVERNMENT OF WORDS—REPETITION.

§ 1. **Preposition.**   The preposition in French is always placed before a noun, a *pronoun*, or a verb in the *infinitive*.

RULE. *All prepositions in French govern the present of the infinitive, whilst they govern the present participle in English.*

Rem. 1. *En* alone is an exception, and requires, as in English, the present participle after it.

Rem. 2. *Après* governs the past or compound infinitive : after reading, *après avoir lu.*

§ 2. **Verbs and Adjectives.**   There is no general rule as to the prepositions required by verbs and adjectives, the preposition varying according to the meaning or relation expressed.   They are indicated in the dictionaries for each particular case.

Still, most adjectives require after them *de* or *à.*

Those requiring *de* generally refer to *abundance* or *scarcity, content* or *discontent, pride* or *shame.*

Those governing *à* generally express an idea of *readiness, inclination, opposition, habit, fitness.*

§ 3. **Repetition of Words.** Articles and adjectives determinative (demonstrative, possessive, indefinite) must be repeated before every noun of a series. The same rule applies to the prepositions (especially *de, à, en*) which are to be repeated before every noun or verb of a series.

V. PLACE OF WORDS—POSSESSIVE CASE.

§ 1. **Adjectives Qualificative** are placed either before or after the noun, but more generally *after* it, especially long adjectives. Those referring to nationality, shape, color, taste, are *always* placed after the noun, also participles used as adjectives.

§ 2. **Adverbs** in French are generally placed after the verb, but NEVER between the subject and the verb, as is frequently the case in English: *Je dis toujours*, I always say. In compound tenses, the adverb comes between the auxiliary and the participle: *J'ai toujours dit.*

Adverbial expressions come last of all, in compound tenses: *Je l'ai fait à dessein.*

§ 3. **Pronouns objects** are placed before the verb, and, in compound tenses, before the auxiliary. The following table (Nos. 3, 4, 5, 6) shows their respective position:

1 Nomin.	2 First Negat.	3 Dative.	4 Acc.	5 Dat. of 3d pers.	6 Genitive Dative.	7	8 2d Neg.	9
Je		me						
Tu		te	le					
Il		se		lui	en			
Elle	ne		la			Aux. verb or verb.	pas	Past participle.
Nous		nous						
Vous		vous	les					
Ils		se						
Elles				leur	y			

§ 4. There is a single exception to this rule: In the imperative *affirmative*, the pronouns objects are placed after the verb; *me, te, se, nous, vous,* come after *le, la, les;* and in that case, *moi* and *toi,* used instead of *me, te,* always come last : *Rendez-la-lui; donnez-le-moi.*

§ 5. The English POSSESSIVE CASE does not exist in French, and the words must be placed in their natural order : my father's sword, *le sabre de mon père ;* the Golden Lion, *le Lion d' Or ;* a small village inn, *une modeste auberge de village.*

§ 6. For other differences in the place of words, see, in the Vocabulary, ENOUGH, SO, SUCH, AGO.

VI. AUXILIARIES.

§ 1. THE principal difference between the two languages as to the use of the auxiliaries in compound tenses, concerns the reflective verb. In French, *all verbs* conjugated *reflectively* take the auxiliary ÊTRE, whilst the auxiliary *to have (avoir)* is used in English: *Je me* SUIS *blessé,* I *have* wounded myself. This rule is without an exception.

§ 2. The English auxiliary verbs *do, did, shall, will, should, would, could, might, may, can, ought,* and *must,* also *to have* and *to be,* form, in answers to questions, many elliptical expressions which have no equivalent in French. In such cases, the chief and predominating idea contained in the question, says Mr. Charente, must be reproduced in the answer, or simply rendered by an interjective word like *en vérité, vraiment, oui, non, peut-être, soit, n'est-ce pas,* or any interjection serving as an equivalent. Have you written? Yes, I have. *Avez-vous écrit?* OUI, J'AI ÉCRIT (or simply OUI). Will you come and see us? I will. *Viendrez-vous nous voir?* CERTAINEMENT.

Who cut that tree? I did. *Qui a coupé cet arbre?*
Moi, or C'est moi.

§ 3. As to the way of rendering in French these auxiliaries, see the Vocabulary for each one.

VII. Use of Tenses.—Imperfect and Past Definite.

§ 1. The French have no progressive tense; consequently, *I read, I am reading, I do read*, are translated by the same tense, the Present Indicative: *Je lis.*

Will and *shall*, as mere auxiliaries, are translated in French by the simple form of the Future; *would* and *should*, by the Conditional.

§ 2. But the stumbling-block with beginners is to discriminate between the Imperfect and the Past definite of the Indicative, as both forms may be expressed by the English Perfect.

Theoretically, the Imperfect is the *descriptive* tense of the French: it expresses a past action, the duration and end of which are not stated. It expresses, also, a *customary*, as well as a *simultaneous*, action or state.

The Past definite is the *narrative* tense of the French: it indicates that an action took place at a time entirely elapsed.[1]

§ 3. Rule. *Practically*, when you have to translate an English Perfect, if, by decomposing it, the sense would necessarily require *did*, use in French the *Past definite*.

If, on the contrary, the sense would require *was* or *were*

---

[1] In familiar conversation and in writing letters, the Past definite is generally replaced by the Past indefinite, which is less formal and can be used whether the time is entirely past or not: *J'ai reçu votre lettre*, or, *je reçus votre lettre.*

with the present participle of the verb, or *used to*, it is the *Imperfect* that must be used.

Incidental or explanatory sentences (side-sentences), generally beginning with a conjunctive, and being usually mere expletives, are mostly to be rendered by the Imperfect.

Ex. ·When I was on the sea-shore, I went bathing nearly every day. One evening, I did not see a shark, swimming towards me ; and, etc.

*Quand j'*ÉTAIS (description ante factum, I was being) *sur le bord de la mer, j'*ALLAIS (I used to go, customary action) *me baigner presque chaque jour. Un soir, je ne* VIS *pas un requin* (narration commences ; we could not well say, *I was not seeing*, but *I did see not*), *qui* NAGEAIT (explanatory sentence, beginning with a conjunctive pronoun) *à ma rencontre.*

§ 4. *Remark.* The *Imperfect* is generally preferred to express a particular opinion or sentiment which is not presented as incontestable: *Il disait que rien ne rendait les mœurs plus aimables que la botanique.* (BERNARDIN DE SAINT-PIERRE.) *On m'a dit ce matin que vous étiez malade.*

VIII. MOODS.

OFTENTIMES, in French as well as in English, transitive verbs have for their *direct object* another verb, or even a whole proposition. Such *verbal objects* are to be rendered either by the *Infinitive*, or by a mood *personal; i.e.* having a subject.

The second verb depends, consequently, for its form and mood, on the first or ruling verb. Hence :

§ 1. RULE. *The second verb is to be put in the* INFINITIVE *in two cases :* 1. *When the two verbs have the same subject, or, in other words, if the same agent acts or suffers in both verbs.* 2. *When the first verb has an indirect object expressed.*

Ex. Cet entrepreneur ne croit pas s'engager, mais je pense qu'il s'engage beaucoup. (In the first part of the sentence, the person who believes and binds himself is the same, *Infinitive;* in the second part, the one who thinks and the one who engages himself *are not* the same person.)

Il nous ordonna de veiller avec soin. (*Ordonner* has an indirect object, which is the subject of the second verb, *Infinitive.*)

Allez chercher vos livres. (The person who *goes* and *seeks for* is the same. It is always the case with the Imperative.)[1]

§ 2. RULE. *But, if neither of these two conditions exists, the second or governed verb is to be put in the* SUBJUNCTIVE, *when there is* DOUBT *or* UNCERTAINTY *in the idea expressed by the first verb.* ANOTHER *mood* (Indicative or Conditional) *is to be used when the first verb expresses an absolute* CERTAINTY.

Je doute qu'il *vienne* (Subj.). Je crois qu'il *viendra* (Fut. Ind.). Croyez-vous qu'il *vienne ?* Sa fille me disait qu'il *serait* bientôt ici.

---

[1] With some French verbs, the Infinitive, though a *direct object*, is sometimes preceded by the preposition à or *de*. In such cases, the preposition plays the part of an article "sui generis," somewhat like *to* before the English Infinitive.

Ex. *Elle aime* λ *rire.* (She likes—what? Joking; direct object.) *L'orateur cessa tout-à-coup* DE *parler.* (The orator ceased—what? to speak, his speech.)

By the above examples, it is easy to see that the preposition à still retains its relation of *inclination, tendency,* and the preposition *de,* that of *separation.*

§ 3. Rule. **Use of the Subjunctive.** *The French Subjunctive, being the mood of* DOUBT *and* UNCERTAINTY, *is to be used :*

After verbs expressing *doubt, desire, command* or *will, supposition, necessity* (namely, *unipersonal* verbs), *fear, apprehension, approval* or *disapproval, grief* or *joy.*

Il faut qu'il VIENNE ; *je doute qu'il* VIENNE ; *je veux qu'il* RESTE *ici ; je crains qu'il ne* SOIT *malade ;* etc.

§ 4. After the following verbs, when used *interrogatively* or *negatively : croire, penser, espérer, s'attendre, s'imaginer, présumer, soupçonner,* etc.

Croyez-vous qu'il VIENNE ? *Je ne pense pas qu'il* VIENNE. But : *J'imagine qu'il arrivera bientôt.*

§ 5. After certain conjunctive locutions : *afin que, pour que, à moins que, avant que, quoique, jusqu'à ce que, pourvu que, c'est assez que, c'est peu que, qui que, quoi que, quel que,* etc.

§ 6. After the superlative absolute : *le meilleur, le moindre, le plus, le mieux, le moins ;* also, *le seul, le premier, le dernier,* when we want to express something doubtful; otherwise the Indicative should be used.[1]

§ 7. Rule. *When the first verb expresses an absolute* CERTAINTY, *use the Indicative or the Conditional.*

IX. Miscellaneous.

§ 1. Though using extensively the passive form of verbs, the French have two favorite ways of rendering

---

[1] There is a kind of uncertainty in our minds when we give to our thought an *interrogative* or *negative* turn ; when we *wish* or *command* something, we do not know if our desire or order will be fulfilled ; it is the uncertainty as to the final result which causes our *fears* and *apprehensions,* etc.

The intelligent student will see at once, from the rules above, that the French subjunctive has very little in common with its English homonym.

some English passive forms, wherever clearness admits of them, and wherever there is a certain vagueness about the agent causing the act or state.

The one consists in the use of the indefinite pronoun *On* (one, they, people) with the verb in the active form, and in the third person singular. The other is the *reflective* form.

Ex. ON *m'a dit,* I was told ; ON *raconte,* they relate, people relate. *Cette règle* SE *trouve,* or, ON *trouve cette règle dans toutes les bonnes grammaires.* This rule is found in all good grammars.

IRREGULAR VERBS

OCCURRING IN THE VOCABULARY.

Acquérir, *j'acquerrai,* j'acquerrais.
to acquire, acquérant, j'acquérais.
avoir. acquis, j'acquis, que j'acquisse.

{ j'acquiers, tu acquiers, il acquiert;
n. acquérons, v. acquérez, ils acquièrent.
q. j'acquière, es, e; q. n. acquérions, iez, qu'ils acquièrent.

Aller, *j'irai,* j'irais.
to go, allant, j'allais.
être. allé, j'allai; que j'allasse.

{ je *vais,* tu *vas,* il *va;*
n. allons, vous allez, ils *vont.*
que j'aille, es, e; q. n. allions, iez, qu'ils aillent.

Asseoir (s'), je *m'assiérai,* je m'assiérais.
to sit down, s'asseyant, je m'asseyais.
être. assis, je m'assis; que je m'assisse.

{ je m'assieds, tu t'assieds, il s'assied·
n. n. asseyons, v. v. asseyez, ils s'asseient.
que je m'asseie, es, e; que n. n. asseyions, iez, qu'ils s'asseient.

Battre, je battrai, je battrais.
to beat, battant, je battais.
avoir. battu, je battis; q. je battisse.

{ je bats, tu bats, il bat;
n. battons, v. battez, ils battent.
q. j. batte, es, e; ions, iez, ent.

Conclure, je conclurai, je conclurais.
to conclude, concluant, je concluais.
avoir. conclu, je conclus; q. je conclusse.

{ je conclus, tu conclus, il conclut;
n. concluons, v. concluez, ils concluent.
q. j. conclue, es, e; ions, iez, ent.

Conduire, je conduirai, je conduirais.
to lead, conduisant, je conduisais.
avoir. conduit, je conduisis; q. je conduisisse.

{ je conduis, tu conduis, il conduit;
n. conduisons, v. conduisez, ils conduisent.
que je conduise, es, e; ions, iez, ent.

Connaître, je connaîtrai, je connaîtrais.
to know, connaissant, je connaissais.
avoir. connu, je connus; que je connusse.

{ je connais, tu connais, il connaît;
n. connaissons, v. connaissez, ils connaissent.
que je connaisse, es, e; ions, iez, ent.

Conquérir, conquérant, conquis, conj. *like*
to conquer. ACQUÉRIR.

Construire, construisant, construit, *like*
to construct. CONDUIRE.

Courir, je *courrai*, je courrais.
to run, courant, je courais.
avoir. couru, je courus; q. je cou-
russe.
{ je cours, tu cours, il court;
n. courons, v. courez, ils cour*ent*.
que je coure, es, e; ions, iez, ent.

Couvrir, je couvrirai, je couvrirais.
to cover, couvrant, je couvrais.
avoir. couvert, je couvris; que je cou-
vrisse.
{ je couvre, tu couvres, il couvre;
n. couvrons, v. couvrez, ils couvr*ent*
que je couvre, es, e; ions, iez, ent.

Craindre, je craindrai, je craindrais.
to fear, craignant, je craignais.
avoir. craint, je *craignis*; q. je crai-
gnisse.
{ je crains, tu crains, il craint;
n. craignons, v. craignez, ils craign*ent*
que je craigne, es, e; ions, iez, ent.

Croire, je croirai, je croirais.
to believe, croyant, je croyais.
avoir. cru, je crus; q. je crusse.
{ je crois, tu crois, il croit;
n. croyons, v. croyez, ils croi*ent*.
que je croie, es, e; q. n. croyions,
iez, qu'ils croient.

Croître, je croîtrai, je croîtrais. ·
to grow, croissant, je croissais.
avoir. cru, je crûs; q. je crusse.
{ je crois, tu crois, il croît;
n. croissons, v. croissez, ils croiss*ent*
q. je croisse, es, e; ions, iez, ent.

Cueillir, je cueillerai, je cueillerais.
to gather, cueillant, je cueillais.
avoir. cueilli, je cueillis; q. je cueil-
lisse.
{ je cueille, tu cueilles, il cueille;
n. cueillons, v. cueillez, ils cueill*ent*.
que je cueille, es, e; ions, iez, ent.

Déchoir, je décherrai, je décherrais.
to decay, ..., je déchoyais.
av. and être. déchu, je déchus; que je dé-
chusse.
{ je déchois, tu déchois, il déchoit;
n. déchoyons, v. déchoyez, ils dé-
choi*ent*.
q. je déchoie, es, e; q. n. déchoyions,
iez, qu'ils déchoient.

Défaillir, (No Fut. no Cond. *Bescherelle*.)
to fail. défaillant, je défaillais.
défailli, je défaillis; que je dé-
faillisse.
{ . . . ., il défaille;
n. défaillons, v. défaillez, ils défaill*ent*.
. . . .

Détruire, détruisant, détruit, *like* CON-
to destroy. DUIRE.

Dire, je dirai, je dirais.
to say. disant, je disais.
avoir. dit, je dis; q. je disse.
{ je dis, tu dis, il dit;
n. disons, v. *dites*, ils dis*ent*.
que je dise, es, e; ions, iez, ent.

Dormir, je dormirai, je dormirais.
to sleep, dormant, je dormais.
avoir. dormi, je dormis; q. je dor-
misse.
{ je dors, tu dors, il dort;
n. dormons, v. dormez, ils dorm*ent*.
que je dorme, es, e; ions, iez, *ent*.

Écrire, j'écrirai, j'écrirais.
to write, écrivant, j'écrivais.
avoir. écrit, *j'écrivis*; que j'écrivisse.
{ j'écris, tu écris, il écrit;
n. écrivons, v. écrivez, ils écriv*ent*.
que j'écrive, es, e; ions, iez, ent.

Envoyer,	*j'enverrai,* j'enverrais.	j'envoie, tu envoies, il envoie ;
to send,	envoyant, j'envoyais.	n. envoyons, v. envoyez, ils envo*ient.*
avoir.	envoyé, j'envoyai ; que j'en-voyasse.	q. j'envoie, es, e ; q. n. envoyions, iez, qu'ils envoient.
Extraire,	j'extrairai, j'extrairais.	j'extrais, tu extrais, il extrait ;
to extract,	extrayant, j'extrayais.	n. extrayons, v. extrayez, ils extra*ient.*
avoir.	extrait, ...	que j'extraie, es, e ; q. n. extrayions, iez, qu'ils extraient.
Faillir,	faillant, failli, *like* DÉFAILLIR.	
to fail.		
Faire,	je *ferai,* je ferais ;	je fais, tu fais, il fait ;
to do,	faisant, je faisais.	n. faisons, v. *faites,* ils *font.*
avoir.	fait, je *fis ;* que je fisse.	q. je *fasse,* es, e ; ions, iez, ent.
Falloir,	il faudra, il faudrait.	(unipersonal) il faut.
to be neces-	fallant, il fallait.	
sary.	fallu, il fallut.	qu'il faille.
avoir.		
Haïr,	je haïrai, je haïrais.	je *hais,* tu *hais,* il *hait ;*
to hate,	haïssant, je haïssais.	n. haïssons, v. haïssez, ils haïss*ent.*
avoir.	haï, je haïs ; que je haïsse.	que je haïsse, es, e ; ions, iez, ent.
Induire,	induisant, induit, *like* CON-DUIRE.	
to induce.		
Inscrire,	inscrivant, inscrit, *like* ÉCRIRE.	
to inscribe.		
Interrompre,	interrompant, interrompu, *like*	
to interrupt.	ROMPRE.	
Joindre,	je joindrai, je joindrais.	je joins, tu joins, il joint ;
to join,	joignant, je joignais.	n. joignons, v. joignez, ils joign*ent.*
avoir.	joint, je *joignis ;* q. je joignisse.	que je joigne, es, e ; ions, iez, ent.
Lire,	je lirai, je lirais.	je lis, tu lis, il lit ;
to read,	lisant, je lisais.	n. lisons, v. lisez, ils lis*ent.*
avoir.	lu, je lus ; que je lusse.	que je lise, es, e ; ions, iez, ent.
Maudire,	je maudirai, je maudirais.	je maudis, tu maudis, il maudit ;
to curse,	maudisant, je maudisais.	n. maudisons, v. maudisez, ils mau-disent.
avoir.	maudit, je maudis ; q. je mau-disse.	que je maudise, es, e ; ions, iez, ent.
Médire,	je médirai, je médirais.	je médis, tu médis, il médit ;
to slander,	médisant, je médisais.	n. médisons, v. médisez, ils médisent.
avoir.	médit, je médis ; q. je médisse.	que je médise, es, e ; ions, iez, ent.
Mettre,	je mettrai, je mettrais.	je mets, tu mets, il met ;
to put,	mettant, je mettais.	n. mettons, v. mettez, ils mett*ent.*
avoir.	mis, je mis ; que je misse.	que je mette, es, e ; ions, iez, ent.
Mourir,	je *mourrai,* je mourrais.	je meurs, tu meurs, il meurt ;
to die,	mourant, je mourais.	n. mourons, v. mourez, ils meur*ent.*
être.	mort, je *mourus ;* q. je mou-russe.	que je meure, es, e ; ions, iez, ent.
Mouvoir,	je *mouvrai,* je mouvrais.	je meus, tu meus, il meut ;
to move,	mouvant, je mouvais.	n. mouvons, v. mouvez, ils meuv*ent.*
avoir.	mu, je mus ; que je musse.	que je meuve, es, e ; mouvions, iez, qu'ils meuvent.

B

3

Naître,	je naîtrai, je naîtrais.	je nais, tu nais, il naît ;
to be born,	naissant, je naissais.	n. naissons, v. naissez, ils naiss*ent.*
être.	né, je *naquis ;* q. je naquisse.	que je naisse, es, e ; ions, iez, ent.
Ouvrir,	ouvrant, ouvert, *like* COUVRIR.	
to open.		
Paraître,	paraissant, paru, *like* CON-	
to appear.	NAÎTRE.	
Partir,	je partirai, je partirais.	je pars, tu pars, il part ;
to depart,	partant, je partais.	n. partons, v. partez, ils part*ent.*
être.	parti, je partis ; q. je partisse.	que je parte, es, e ; ions, iez, enL
Peindre,	peignant, peint, *like* CRAINDRE.	
to paint.		
Plaindre,	plaignant, plaint, *like* CRAIN-	
to pity.	DRE.	
Plaire,	je plairai, je plairais.	je plais, tu plais, il plaît ;
to please,	plaisant, je plaisais.	n. plaisons, v. plaisez, ils plais*ent.*
avoir.	plu, je plus ; q. je plusse.	que je plaise, es, e ; ions, iez, ent.
Pourvoir,	je pourvoirai, je pourvoirais.	je pourvois, tu pourvois, il pourvoit ;
to provide,	pourvoyant, je pourvoyais.	n. pourvoyons, v. pourvoyez, ils pour-
avoir.	pourvu, je pourvus ; que je pourvusse.	voi*ent.*
		que je pourvoie, es, e ; q. n. pourvoyions, iez, qu'ils pourvoient.
Pouvoir,	je *pourrai,* je pourrais.	je puis or je peux, tu peux, il peut ;
to be able,	pouvant, je pouvais.	n. pouvons, v. pouvez, ils peuvent.
avoir.	pu, je pus ; q. je pusse.	que je puisse, es, e ; ions, iez, ent.
Prendre,	je prendrai, je prendrais.	je prends, tu prends, il prend ;
to take,	prenant, je prenais.	n. prenons, v. prenez, ils prenn*ent.*
avoir.	pris, je pris ; q. je prisse.	que je prenne, es, e ; ions, iez, ent.
Prévoir,	je prévoirai, je prévoirais.	je prévois, tu prévois, il prévoit ;
to foresee,	prévoyant, je prévoyais.	n. prévoyons, v. prévoyez, ils pré-
avoir.	prévu, je prévis ; que je prévisse.	voi*ent.*
		q. je prévoie, es, e ; q. n. prévoyions, iez. qu'ils prévoi*ent.*
Repentir (se),	je me repentirai ;—rais.	je me repens, tu te repens, il se re-
to repent,	se repentant, je me repentais.	pent ;
être.	repenti, je me repentis ;—isse.	n. n. repentons, v. v. repentez, ils se repent*ent.*
		que je me repente, es, e ; ions, iez, ent.
Rire,	je rirai, je rirais.	je ris, tu ris, il rit ;
to laugh,	riant, je riais.	n. rions, v. riez, ils ri*ent.*
avoir.	ri, je ris ; que je risse.	que je rie, es, e ; rions, riez, ent.
Rompre,	je romprai, je romprais.	je romps, tu romps, il rompt ;
to break,	rompant, je rompais.	n. rompons, v. rompez, ils romp*ent.*
avoir.	rompu, je rompis ; q. je rompisse.	que je rompe, es, e ; ions, iez, eut.
Savoir,	je saurai, je saurais.	je sais, tu sais, il sait ;
to know,	sachant, je *savais.*	n. savons, v. savez, ils savent.
avoir.	su. je sus ; que je susse.	que je *sache,* es, e ; ions, iez, ent.

Séduire, séduisant, séduit, *like* CON-
to seduce. DUIRE.

Sentir, je sentirai, je sentirais. je sens, tu sens, il sent ;
to feel, sentant, je sentais. n. sentons, v. sentez, ils sent*ent.*
avoir. senti, je sentis ; q. je sentisse. que je sente, es, e ; ions, iez, ent.

Servir, je servirai, je servirais. je sers, tu sers, il sert ;
to serve, servant, je servais. n. servons, v. servez, ils serv*ent.*
avoir. servi, je servis ; q. je servisse. que je serve, es, e ; ions, iez, ent.

Sortir, sortant, sorti, *like* PARTIR.
to go out.

Souffrir, souffrant, souffert, *like* OUVRIR.
to suffer.

Suivre, je suivrai, je suivrais. je suis, tu suis, il suit ;
to follow, suivant, je suivais. n. suivons, v. suivez, ils suiv*ent.*
avoir. suivi, je suivis ; q. je suivisse. que je suive, es, e ; ions, iez, ent.

Taire (se), se taisant, tu, *like* PLAIRE.
to be silent.

Tenir, je *tiendrai,* je tiendrais. je tiens, tu tiens, il tient ;
to hold, tenant, je tenais. n. tenons, v. tenez, ils tienn*ent.*
avoir. tenu, je *tins ;* q. je tinsse. que je tienne, es, e ; ions, iez, ent.

Traduire, traduisant, traduit, *like* CON-
to translate. DUIRE.

Tressaillir, tressaillant, tressailli, *like* DÉ-
to be startled. FAILLIR.

Vaincre, je vaincrai, je vaincrais. je vaincs, tu vaincs, il vainc ;
to conquer, vainquant, je vainquais. n. vainquons, v. vainquez, ils vain-
avoir. vaincu, je *vainquis ;* que je quent.
vainquisse. que je vainque, es, e ; ions, iez, ent.

Valoir, je *vaudrai,* je vaudrais. je vaux, tu vaux, il vaut ;
to be worth, valant, je valais. n. valons, v. valez, ils valent.
avoir. valu, je valus ; q. je valusse. q. je *vaille,* es, e ; q. n. valions, iez,
qu'ils *vaillent.*

Venir, je *viendrai,* je viendrais. je viens, tu viens, il vient ;
to come, venant, je venais. n. venons, v. venez, ils vienn*ent.*
être. venu, je *vins ;* q. je vinsse. que je vienne, es, e ; q. n. venions,
iez, qu'ils viennent.

Vêtir (se), je me vêtirai, je me vêtirais. je me vêts, tu te vêts, il se vêt ;
to clothe, se vêtant, je me vêtais. n. n. vêtons, v. v. vêtez, ils se vêt*ent.*
être. vêtu, je me vêtis ; q. je me vê- que je me vête, es, e ; ions, iez, ent.
tisse.

Voir, je *verrai,* je verrais. je vois, tu vois, il voit ;
to see, voyant, je voyais. n. voyons, v. voyez, ils voi*ent.*
avoir. vu, je *vis ;* que je visse. que je voie, es, e ; q. n. voyions, iez,
qu'ils voient.

Vouloir, je voudrai, je voudrais. je veux, tu veux, il veut ;
to be willing, voulant, je voulais. n. voulons, v. voulez, ils veulent.
avoir. voulu, je voulus ; q. je vou- que je veuille, es, e ; q. n. voulions,
lusse. iez, qu'ils veuillent.

PART SECOND.

THE LADY OF LYONS.

ADEQUATE VOCABULARY.

ABBREVIATIONS AND REFERENCES.

In the Text of the Play:

I. The MARGINAL NUMBERS divide the text into sections of about ten lines, each section being complete in itself. One or two sections may be given, at will, for each exercise.

II. A STAR (*) following a word notifies the student that he must read in the Vocabulary all that concerns that word, as some idiomatical difficulty will there be explained.

III. APOSTROPHES, single or double (' "), at the end of certain nouns or adjectives, indicate that such words are not to be found in the Vocabulary, as they are *alike* in spelling and *meaning* in both languages. A single apostrophe indicates the masculine gender, a double apostrophe the feminine. Thus :—

> miracle ' = masculine noun.   Intention " = feminine noun.
> constant ' = masculine form of the French adjective.
> clandestine ", active " = feminine form of the French adjective.

IV. A double dagger (‡) stands for the conjunction THAT or the preposition TO omitted in English, but always to be rendered in French : THAT by *que*, and TO by *à*.[1] In stage directions, ‡ stands for the subject to be expressed in French, whilst understood in English.

V. A number (1, 2, 3, etc.) after a word, either in the text of the Play or in the Vocabulary, refers to one of the nine chapters of the Synopsis. If, occasionally, two numbers are given, the first refers to the chapter, and the second to a particular paragraph of that chapter.

INDEX OF THE SYNOPSIS.

---

[1] The preposition *à* is understood in French only when the objective pronoun *lui* or *leur* is to be placed before the verb (dative case).

(31)

LADY OF LYONS.

[FECHTER'S VERSION.]

ACT I.

1. SCENE I.—*The exterior of a small Village* [55] *Inn—sign the Golden Lion'—a few leagues from Lyons, which is seen* [9] *at a distance**.

Beauseant (*without*, R.). Yes, you may * bait the horses; we shall rest here an hour.

Enter BEAUSEANT *and* GLAVIS, R.

Glavis. Really, my dear Beauseant, consider that I have promised to spend * a day or two with you at your chateau'—that I am quite at your mercy for my entertainment—and yet you are as * silent and gloomy as a mute at a funeral, or an Englishman at a party * of pleasure.

Beauseant. Bear * with me.—The fact is, that I am miserable !

Glavis. You—the richest and gayest bachelor in * Lyons ?

Beauseant. It is * because I am a * bachelor that I am miserable'. **2.** ═ Thou knowest Pauline''—the only daughter of the' rich merchant, Mons. Deschappelles'?

Glavis. Know her !—Who does [6] not ?—as pretty as Venus'' and as proud as Juno.

Beauseant. Her * taste is worse than her pride—(*draw-*

B*

ing himself up).   Know, Glavis',‡ she has actually refused
*me ?*⁵

Glavis (aside). So* she has⁶ me !—very consoling ! in
all cases of heart-ache, the application of another man's⁵
disappointment draws out the pain, and allays the irrita-
tion ".—(*Aloud.*) Refused you !⁵ and wherefore?

Beauseant. I know not, unless it be* because the
Revolution" swept away my father's⁵ title of marquis '—and
she will* not marry a commoner. **3.**=Now, as* we have
no noblemen left* in France, as we are all citizens, and
equals, she can only hope, that, in spite of the war, some
English Milord or German count will risk his life by* coming to Lyons and making her⁵⁶ my lady. Refused me,⁵ and
with scorn !—By heaven, I'll not submit to it tamely—I'm
in a perfect * fever of mortification " and rage".—Refused
me, indeed !

Glavis. Be comforted, my dear fellow *—I will tell you⁵
a secret'.   For the same reason she refused ME !⁵

Beauseant. You!—that's* a very different ' matter;
but give me⁵ your hand, Glavis '—we'll think of some
plan ' to humble her.⁵   By Jove, I should⁶ like to see her⁵
married to a strolling⁵ player !

4. *Enter** LANDLORD *and his* DAUGHTER, *from the Inn,*
L. D. *in* F.

Landlord. Your servant, citizen Beauseant—servant,
sir.   Perhaps you will take* dinner before you proceed
to your chateau'; our larder is most plentifully supplied.

Beauseant. I have no appetite.

Glavis. Nor* I.   Still it is bad travelling * on an empty
stomach.   Come, landlord, let's see your bill.   What
have you got ? * [*Takes and looks over bill of fare.   Shout
without*]   "Long* live the Prince' !—Long live the
Prince' ! "

Beauseant. The Prince!—what Prince is that? I thought we had no princes left* in France.

Landlord. Ha ha! the lads always⁵ call him Prince. He has just * won the prize in a shooting-match, and they are taking⁷ him home in triumph.

Beauseant. Him! and who's Mr. Him?

5. *Landlord.* Who should he * be, but the pride of the village', Claude' Melnotte'?—of course you have heard of Claude Melnotte?

Glavis (giving back the bill of fare). Never had that honor. Soup—ragout' of hare—roast chicken—and, in short, all ‡ you have !

Beauseant. The son of old Melnotte² the gardener?

Landlord. Exactly so—a wonderful young man !

Beauseant. How wonderful?—are his cabbages bettei than other people's?⁵

Landlord. Nay, he doesn't garden any more; his father left him well off.*   He's only a genus.

Glavis. A what?

Landlord. A genus!—a man who can do every thing in life,² except anything that's useful;—that's a genus.

Beauseant. You raise my curiosity—proceed.

6. *Landlord.* Well then, about four years ago, old Melnotte died, and left⁷ his son well * -to-do in the world. We then⁵ all observed⁷ that a great change came⁷ over young Claude;² he took⁷ to reading and Latin, and hired⁷ a professor from Lyons, who had so * much in his head that he was⁷ forced to wear a great full-bottom wig to cover it.   Then he took a fencing-master, and a dancing-master, and a music-master, and then he learned⁷ to paint; and at last it was said⁹ that young Claude was * to go to Paris and set * up for a painter.   The lads laughed⁷ at him at first; but he is a stout fellow, is Claude, and as brave' as a lion', and soon taught them to laugh * the wrong side of their mouths; and now all the boys swear by him, and all the girls pray for him.

7. *Beauseant.* A promising youth, certainly ! And why do they call him prince' ?

Landlord. Partly because he is at the head of them all, and partly because he has such a proud way with * him, and wears such fine clothes—and, in short—looks like a prince.

Beauseant. And what could* have turned the foolish fellow's⁵ brain ? The Revolution', I suppose.

Landlord. Yes—the Revolution' that turns us all topsy-* turvy—the revolution of Love.

Beauseant. Romantic young Corydon' ! And with whom is he in love? *

Landlord. Why—but it is a secret', gentlemen.

Beauseant. Oh! certainly.

8. *Landlord.* Why, then, I hear from his mother, good soul !* that it is no less* a person than the beauty of Lyons, Pauline'' Deschappelles'.

Beauseant and Glavis. Ha ! ha ! Capital !

Landlord. You may laugh, but it is as true as I stand here.

Beauseant. And what does the beauty of Lyons say* to his suit?

Landlord. Lord, sir, she never⁵ even condescended to look at him ; though when he* was a boy he worked in her father's⁵ garden.

Beauseant. Are you sure of that?

Landlord. His mother says that Mademoiselle' does not know * him by sight.*

Beauseant (taking GLAVIS *aside).* I have hit it—I have hit it ;—here* is our revenge ! Here is a prince for our haughty damsel. Do you take* me ?

Glavis. Deuce take me if I do !⁶

9. *Beauseant.* Blockhead !—it's as* clear as a map.* What if we could* make * this elegant' clown pass himself off as a foreign prince'? lend him money, clothes, equipage' for the purpose?—make him propose* to Pauline?—marry Pauline? Would it not be delicious?

Glavis. Ha! ha!—excellent'! But how shall we support the necessary expenses of his* highness?

Beauseant. Pshaw! Revenge is worth a much larger* sacrifice' than a few hundred louis'; as for details', my valet' is the truest* fellow in* the world, and we shall have the appointment of his highness's establishment. Let's go to him at once, and see if he be⁸ really this Admirable' Crichton'.

Glavis. With all my heart ;*—but the dinner?

10. *Beauseant.* Always thinking of dinner! Hark ye, landlord, how far is it to young Melnotte's⁵ cottage? I should like to see such* a prodigy.

Landlord. Turn down the lane, then strike across the common, and you will see his mother's⁵ cottage.

Beauseant. True, he lives with his mother.—(*aside.*) We will not trust to an old woman's⁵ discretion''; better* send for him hither, or try to see him alone. Come, Glavis.

Glavis. Yes,—Beauseant, Glavis and Co., manufacturers of princes, wholesale and retail,*—an uncommonly genteel line of business. But why so grave?

Beauseant. You think only of the sport—I of the revenge. [*Exeunt within the Inn,* D. *in* F.

4

11. Scene II.—*The interior of* Melnotte's[5] *cottage; flowers placed here and there; a guitar on an oaken[5] table"*, *with a portfolio, etc.; a picture on an easel, covered by a curtain; fencing-foils crossed* over the mantel-piece; an attempt at refinement in spite of the homeliness of the fur- niture, etc.; a staircase to the right conducts to the upper story.**

(*Shout * without*, R. U. E.) "Long* live Claude Mel- notte! Long live the Prince!"

Widow Melnotte. Hark!—there's* my dear son; car- ried off the prize, I'm sure"; and now he'll want to treat them all.

Claude Melnotte (opening the door). What, you won't come .in, my friends? Well, well, there's * a trifle to * make merry elsewhere. Good day to you all,—good day!—(*Shout.*) "Hurrah! Long live prince Claude!"

12. *Enter* Claude Melnotte, L. D. *in* F., *with a rifle in his hand.*

Melnotte. Give me joy,* dear mother! I've won the prize! never missed one shot! Is it not handsome, this gun?

Widow. Humph! Well, what is it worth, Claude?

Melnotte. Worth! What is a ribbon worth to a soldier? Worth—everything! Glory is priceless!

Widow. Leave glory to great folks.* Ah! Claude, Claude! castles in the air cost a vast deal to keep up! How is all* this to end? What good does it do thee to learn Latin, and sing songs, and play on the guitar, and fence, and dance, and paint pictures? all very fine; but what does it bring in?

13. *Melnotte.* Wealth! wealth, my mother!—wealth

to the mind—wealth to the heart—high thoughts—bright
dreams—the hope of fame—the ambition '' to be worthier
to love Pauline.

Widow. My poor son !—the young lady will never ⁵
think of thee.

Melnotte. Do the stars think of us? Yet if the prisoner see them shine ⁸ in his dungeon, wouldst thou bid
him turn away from *their* lustre? Even from this low
cell, poverty,—I lift my * eyes to Pauline and forget my
chains. (‡ *Goes to the picture and draws aside the curtain.*)
See, this * is her image—painted from memory.—Oh, how
the canvas wrongs her ! (*Takes up the brush and throws it
aside.*) I shall never be a painter. I can paint no likeness but one, and that is above all art '. **14.**=I would
turn * soldier—France ² needs soldiers ! But to leave the
air' that Pauline breathes ! What is the hour?—so late !
I will tell thee a secret ', mother. Thou knowest not that
for the last * six weeks I have sent every day the rarest flowers to Pauline ; she wears them. I have seen them on her
breast. Ah ! and then the whole universe seemed⁷ filled
with odors ! I have now grown * more bold—I have
poured * my worship into poetry—I have sent my verses
to Pauline—I have signed * them with my own name.
My messenger ought to be back by this time. I bade⁷
him wait for an answer.

15. *Widow.* And what answer do you expect, Claude?

Melnotte. That which the Queen of Navarre '' sent to
the' poor troubadour :—'' Let me see the Oracle' that can
tell ‡nations '' ‡ I am beautiful !'' She will admit me.
I shall hear her speak *—I shall meet her eyes—I shall
read upon her cheek the sweet thoughts that translate *
themselves into blushes. Then, then, oh, then,—she may
forget that I am the peasant's ⁵ son !

Widow. Nay, if * she will but hear thee talk,* Claude !

Melnotte. I foresee* it all. She will tell me that desert
is the true rank. She will give me a badge—a flower—a
glove! Oh, rapture! **16.**=I shall join the armies of
the Republic—I shall rise—I shall win* a name that
beauty will not blush to hear. I shall return with the
right to say to her—" See how love² does·not level the
proud, but raise the humble !" Oh, how my heart swells*
within me !—Oh, what glorious Prophets of the Future
are Youth² and Hope²!   [*Knock at the door* D. *in* F.
Widow. Come in.

Enter GASPAR, D. *in* F.

Melnotte. Welcome, Gaspar, welcome. Where is the
letter? Why do you turn away, man?* where is the
letter? (GASPAR *gives*‡ *him one.**) This—this is mine,*
the one‡ I intrusted to thee. Didst thou not leave it?

Gaspar. Yes, I left⁷ it.

Melnotte. My own verses returned⁹ to me ! Nothing
else? *

17. *Gaspar.* Thou wilt be proud to hear how thy
messenger was honored. For thy sake,* Melnotte, I have
borne that which no Frenchman can bear without disgrace.

Melnotte. Disgrace, Gaspar ! Disgrace ?

Gaspar. I gave thy letter to the porter, who passed it
from lackey to lackey till it reached the lady it was mea⁻t *
for.

Melnotte. It reached her, then ;—are you sure of that ?
It reached her,—well, well !

Gaspar. It reached her, and was returned to me with
blows. Dost hear, Melnotte? with blows !² Death !
are we slaves still, that we are to be thus dealt * with, we
peasants ?²

18. *Melnotte.* With blows? No, Gaspar, no ; not*
blows?

Gaspar. I could * show thee⁵ the marks, if * it were not so deep a shame to bear them.   The lackey who tossed thy letter into the mire, swore⁷ that his lady and her mother never were so insulted.⁹   What could * thy letter contain, Claude ?

Melnotte (looking over the letter). Not a line that a serf might not have written to an empress.   No, not one !

Gaspar. They⁹ promise thee the same greeting ‡ they gave me, if * thou wilt pass that way.*   Shall we endure this, Claude ?

Melnotte (wringing GASPAR'S *hand).* Forgive me ; the fault was mine,* I have brought * this on thee ; I will not forget it ; thou shalt be avenged !   The heartless insolence !

19. *Gaspar.* Thou art moved, Melnotte ; think not of me ; I would go through fire² and water⁴³ to serve thee ; but—a blow !   It is not the *bruise* that galls,—it is the *blush*, Melnotte !

Melnotte. Say,* what message' ? How insulted ? Wherefore ?   What the offence ?

Gaspar. Did you not write to Pauline Deschappelles, the daughter of the rich merchant ?

Melnotte. Well ?

Gaspar. Are you not a peasant—a gardener's⁵ son ?— that was the offence.   Sleep * on it, Melnotte.   Blows² to a French citizen ! blows !   [*Exit* D. *in* F.

Widow. Now you are cured, Claude !

20. *Melnotte (tearing the letter).* So * do I scatter her image to the winds—I will stop her in the open streets * —I will insult her—I will beat her menial ruffians—I will —(‡*turns suddenly to* WIDOW²).   Mother, am I humpbacked—deformed—hideous?

Widow. You !

Melnotte. A coward—a thief—a liar ?

Widow. You !

Melnotte. Or a dull fool—a vain, drivelling, brainless idiot?

Widow. No, no.

Melnotte. What am I, then—worse* than all these? Why, I am a peasant! What has a peasant to do with love? Vain' Revolutions", why lavish your cruelty on the great? Oh, that we,—we the hewers of wood and drawers of water, had been swept away, so that the proud might* learn what the world would be without us!—

Enter BEAUSEANT, D. *in* F., *mysteriously.*

21. *Beauseant (taking him aside).* Young man, I know thy secret—thou lovest above thy station. If thou hast wit,² courage", and discretion", I can secure to thee the realization of thy most sanguine* hopes; and the sole condition"‡ I ask in return is, that thou shalt be steadfast to thine own ends. I shall demand from thee a solemn oath to marry her whom thou lovest; to bear her to thine own home on thy wedding* night. I am serious.*

Melnotte. Can I believe my ears? Are our own passions" the sorcerers that raise up for us spirits of good² or evil?²

Widow. Who is this, Claude?

22. *Melnotte.* "Marry her whom thou lovest"—"bear her to thine own home,"—O, revenge and love! which of you is the stronger?—*(gazing on the picture.)* Sweet face, thou smilest on me from the canvas; weak fool that I am, do I then love her still? No, it is the vision" of my own romance that I have worshipped; it is the reality to which I bring scorn for scorn.—Adieu', mother; I will return anon. My brain reels—the earth swims before me.—No, it is *not** mockery; I do not dream!

Beauseant. I will be revenged now!

END OF ACT I.

ACT II.

23. SCENE I.—*The Gardens of* M. DESCHAPPELLES'[5] *House at Lyons—the House seen*[9'] *at the back of the Stage.*

Enter BEAUSEANT *and* GLAVIS *from the House,* L. S. E.

Beauseant. Well, what* think you of my plot? Has it not succeeded to a miracle?* The instant that I introduced his Highness, the Prince of Como, to the pompous mother and the scornful daughter, it was all over* with them; he came[7]—he saw—he conquered; and, though it is* not many days since he arrived, they have already promised him the hand of Pauline.

Glavis. It is lucky,* though, that you told them‡ his Highness travelled[7] incognito, for fear* the Directory[3] (who are[3] not very fond of princes) should lay him by the heels: for he has a wonderful wish to keep up his rank, and scatters our gold about with as much coolness as if he were[7] watering his own flower-pots.

24. *Beauseant.* True, he is damnably extravagant; I think the sly dog does it out* of malice". However, it must be owned that he reflects* credit on his loyal subjects, and makes a very pretty* figure" in his fine clothes with my diamond[5] snuff-box.

Glavis. And my diamond[5] ring! But do you think that he will be firm to the last?* I fancy I see symptoms[π] of relenting: he will never keep up his rank, if he once let out his conscience".

Beauseant. His oath binds him; he cannot retreat without[4] being forsworn, and those low fellows are always superstitious! But, as it is,* I tremble lest* he be dis-

covered; that bluff Colonel Damas (Madame Deschappelles' ⁵ cousin) evidently suspects him; **25.**＝we must
make haste and conclude the farce; I have thought of a
plan to end it this very* day.

Glavis. This very day! Poor Pauline! her dream will
be soon over. *

Beauseant. Yes, this day they shall be married;* this
evening, according to his oath, he shall carry his bride to
the Golden Lion, and then pomp, equipage', retinue,
and title, all shall vanish at once; and her Highness the
Princess shall find that she has refused the son of a Marquis', to marry the son of a gardener.—Oh, Pauline!
once loved, now hated, yet still not relinquished, thou
shalt drain* the cup to the dregs,—thou shalt know what
it is to be humbled!

Enter, from the House, L. S. E., MELNOTTE *as* the Prince
of Como, leading in* PAULINE; MADAME DESCHAPPELLES
fanning herself; and Colonel DAMAS.

26. BEAUSEANT *and* GLAVIS *bow respectfully.* PAULINE
and MELNOTTE *walk apart.*

Madame Deschap. Good-morning, gentlemen; really
I am so fatigued with laughter, the dear Prince' is so entertaining. What wit* he has! any one might see that
he has spent his whole life in courts. ⁹

Damas. And what the deuce do you know about
courts, ⁹ cousin' Deschappelles? You women regard
men just as you buy books—you never care what is in*
them, but how they are bound and lettered. 'Sdeath, I
don't think you would even look at your Bible'', if it
had not a title to it.

27. *Madame Deschap.* How coarse you are, cousin'
Damas!—quite the manners of a barrack—you don't deserve to be one of our family; really we must drop your

acquaintance when Pauline marries. I cannot patronize
any relations that would discredit my future son-in-law,
the Prince of Como.

Melnotte (advancing). These* are beautiful gardens, Madame". (BEAUSEANT *and* GLAVIS *retire.*) Who planned
them?

Madame Deschap. A gardener named Melnotte, your
Highness—an honest* man who knew[73] his station. I
can't say as much* for his son—a presuming fellow,* who
—ha! ha!—actually wrote[7] verses—such doggerel!—to
my daughter.

Pauline. Yes—how you would have laughed at them,
Prince—*you* who write[3] such beautiful verses!

28. *Melnotte.* This Melnotte must be a monstrous impudent person!

Damas. Is he good-looking?

Madame Deschap. I never notice such *canaille* "—an
ugly, mean-looking clown, if I remember* right.

Damas. Yet I heard your porter say ‡ he was wonderfully like his Highness.

Melnotte (taking snuff). You are complimentary.

Madame Deschap. For shame, cousin Damas!—like the
Prince, indeed!

Pauline. Like you! Ah, mother,* like our beautiful
Prince! I'll never speak to you again, cousin Damas.

Melnotte (aside). Humph!—rank is a great beautifier!
I never passed for an Apollo while I was a peasant; if I
am so handsome as a prince', what should I be as an emperor? **29.**=(*aloud.*) Monsieur' Beauseant', will you
honor me?   ‡ [*Offers snuff.*

Beauseant. No, your Highness, I have no small vices".

Melnotte. Nay, if it were a vice' you'd be sure to have
it, Monsieur Beauseant.

Madame Deschap. Ha! ha!—how very severe! *—
what wit!

Beauseant (in a rage" and aside). Curse his impertinence"!

Madame Deschap. What * a superb snuff-box!

Pauline. And what a* beautiful ring!

Melnotte. You like the box—a trifle—interesting perhaps from associations—a present from Louis XIV. to my
great-great-grandmother. Honor me by⁴ accepting it.

Beauseant (plucking him by the sleeve). How!—what
the devil! My box!—are you mad? It is worth five
hundred * louis '.

30. *Melnotte (unheeding him, and turning to* PAULINE).
And you like * this ring! Ah, it has indeed a lustre since
your eyes have shone on it (*placing* * *it on her finger*).
Henceforth hold * me, sweet enchantress, the Slave of the
Ring.

Glavis (pulling him). Stay, stay—what are you about?*
My maiden aunt's⁵ legacy—a diamond of the first water.*
You shall be hanged for swindling, sir.

Melnotte (pretending * *not to hear*). It is curious, this
ring: it is the one* with which my grandfather, the Doge'
of Venice, married the Adriatic!

[MADAME *and* PAULINE *examine the ring.*

31. *Melnotte (to* BEAUSEANT *and* GLAVIS). Fie, gentlemen, princes' must be generous!—(*Turns to* DAMAS, *who
watches them closely*). These kind friends have my interest so much at heart,* that they are as careful of my
property as if* it were their own.*

Beauseant and Glavis (confusedly). Ha! ha!—very
good joke that!

[*Appear to remonstrate with* MELNOTTE *in dumb* * *show.*

Damas. What's all that whispering?⁸ I am sure ‡
there is some juggle here; hang me if I think ‡ he is an

Italian, after all. 'Gad! I'll try him. Servitore umi-
lissimo, Excellenza.[1]

Melnotte. Hum—what does he mean, I wonder?

Damas. Godo di vedervi in buona salute.[2]

Melnotte. Hem—hem!

Damas. Fa bel tempo—che si dice di nuovo?[3]

Melnotte. Well, Sir, what's all that gibberish?

32. *Damas.* Oh, oh!—only Italian, your Highness!
—The prince of Como does not understand his own
language!

Melnotte. Not as you pronounce it: who the deuce
could?[6]

Madame Deschap. Ha! ha! cousin Damas, never pretend* to what you don't know.

Pauline. Ha! ha! cousin' Damas'; *you* speak Italian,
indeed!   [*Makes a mocking gesture* at him.

Beauseant (*to* GLAVIS). Clever dog!*—how ready!*

Glavis. Ready, yes; with my diamond ring!—Damn
his readiness!

Damas. Laugh at me!—laugh at a colonel' in* the
French army!—The fellow's an impostor; I know ‡ he* is.
I'll see if he understands fighting[8] as well as he does[4]
Italian—**33.**=(*Goes up to him, and aside.*) Sir, you are a
jackanapes! Can you construe that?

Melnotte. No, sir! I never construe affronts' in the
presence" of ladies; by-and-by I shall be happy to take
a lesson—or give one.*

Damas. I'll find the occasion", never fear!*

Madame Deschap. Where are you going, cousin'?

---

[1] Your Excellency's most humble servant.
[2] I am glad to see you in good health.
[3] Fine weather. What news is there?

Damas. To correct my Italian. [*Exit into House,* L. S. E

Beauseant (to GLAVIS). Let us after,* and pacify him ; he evidently suspects something.

Glavis. Yes !—but my diamond⁵ ring ?

Beauseant. And my box !—We are over-taxed,* fellow-subject !*—we must stop the supplies, and dethrone the Prince'.

Glavis. Prince !— he ought to be heir-apparent to King⁹ Stork !   [*Exeunt into House,* L. S. E.

34. *Madame Deschap.* Dare I ask your Highness to forgive my cousin's⁵ insufferable vulgarity?

Pauline. Oh, yes!—you will forgive his manner for the sake* of his heart.

Melnotte. And for the sake of his cousin'. Ah, Madam, there is one comfort in rank—we are so sure of our position" that we are not easily affronted. Besides, M. Damas has bought the right of indulgence" from his friends,* by⁴ never⁵ showing it to his enemies.

Pauline. Ah ! he is, indeed, as brave' in action" as he is rude in speech. He rose* from the ranks to his present grade',—and in two years.

Melnotte. In two years !—two years, did you say ?

Madame Deschap. (aside). I don't like leaving girls alone with their lovers ; but with a prince, it* would be so ill-bred to be prudish ! [*Exit into House,* L. S. E.

35. *Melnotte.* You can be proud of your connection with one who owes his position" to merit,—not birth.

Pauline. Why, yes ; but still—

Melnotte. Still what, Pauline?

Pauline. There is something glorious in the Heritage' of Command. A man who has ancestors is like a Representative of the Past.

Melnotte. True ;* but, like other representatives, nine times out of ten he is a silent member.* Ah, Pauline !

not to the Past, but to the Future, looks true nobility,
and finds its blazon in posterity.

Pauline. You say this to please me, who have³ no ancestors; but you, Prince, must be proud of so* illustrious
a race!

36. *Melnotte.* No, no! I would⁶ not, were* I fifty
times a prince, be a pensioner on the Dead! I honor
birth and ancestry when they are regarded as the incen-
tives to exertion, not the title-deeds to sloth! I honor the
laurels that overshadow the graves of our fathers. It is*
our fathers‡ I emulate, when I desire that beneath the
evergreen ‡ I myself have planted, my own ashes may repose! Dearest, couldst* thou but see with my eyes!

Pauline. I cannot forego pride when I look on thee
and think that thou lovest me. Sweet Prince, tell me
again of thy palace by the lake of Como; it is* so pleasant to hear of thy splendors, since* thou didst swear to
me that they would be desolate without Pauline; and
when thou describest them, it is with a mocking lip and
a noble scorn, as* if custom had made thee disdain
greatness.

37. *Melnotte.* Nay, dearest, nay, if thou wouldst have*
 me paint
The home to which, could Love fulfil* its prayers,
This hand would lead thee, listen!* A deep vale,

---

* The reader will observe that Melnotte evades the request of Pauline.
He proceeds to describe a home, which he does not say he possesses,
but to which he would lead her, *"could love fulfil its prayers."* This
caution is intended as a reply to a sagacious critic who censures the
description because it is not an exact and prosaic inventory of the char-
acteristics of the lake of Como!—When Melnotte, for instance, talks of
birds, "that syllable the name of Pauline" (by the way, a literal translation from an Italian poet), he is not thinking of ornithology, but probably
of the Arabian Nights. He is venting the extravagant, but natural, en-
thusiasm of the Poet and the Lover.

C 5

Shut out by Alpine hills from the rude world,
Near a clear lake, margined by fruits of gold
And whispering* myrtles; glassing softest skies
As* cloudless, save* with rare and roseate shadows,
As I would have* thy fate!

    Pauline. My own* dear love!

38. *Melnotte.* A palace lifting* to eternal summer
Its marble⁵ walls, from out a glossy bower
Of coolest foliage musical with birds,
Whose songs should syllable thy name! At noon
We sit beneath the arching vines, and wonder*
Why Earth could be unhappy, while the Heavens
Still left us youth²¹ and love! We'd have no friends²⁹
That* were not lovers; no ambition", save*
To excel them all in love; we'd read no books
That were not tales of love—that we might smile
To think* how poorly eloquence" of words
Translates the poetry of hearts like ours!

39. And when night came, amidst the breathless heavens
We'd guess what star should* be our home when love
Becomes immortal;* while the perfumed light
Stole* through the mists of alabaster lamps,
And every air* was heavy with the sighs
Of orange⁵ groves and music from sweet lutes,
And murmurs of low fountains that gush forth
I' the midst of roses" !—Dost thou like the picture?*

    Pauline. Oh! as the bee upon the flower, I hang
Upon the honey of thy eloquent' tongue!
Am I not blest? And if I love too wildly,
Who would not love thee, like Pauline?

40. *Melnotte* (*bitterly*). Oh false one!*
It is the *prince'* thou lovest, not the *man;*
If in the stead of luxury, pomp,⁴³ and power,
I had painted poverty, and toil, and care,

Thou hadst found no honey on my tongue ;--Pauline,
That is not love!

Pauline. Thou wrong'st me, cruel' Prince'!
'Tis * true I might not at the first been won,
Save through the weakness of a flattered pride;
But *now !*—Oh! trust me,—couldst thou fall from power,
And sink——

Melnotte. As low as that poor gardener's⁵ son
Who dared to lift* his eyes to thee?

41. *Pauline.* Even then,
Methinks thou wouldst be only made* more dear
By the sweet thought that I could prove how* deep
Is woman's⁵ love! We are like the insects, caught
By the poor glittering of a garish flame!
But oh, the wings once scorched,—the brightest star
Lures us no more ; and by the fatal light
We cling till death!

Melnotte. Angel!

(*Aside.*) O conscience"! conscience!
It must * not be!—her love hath grown * a torture
Worse than her hate. I will at once to Beauseant,
And——ha! he comes.——Sweet love, one moment leave
        me.
I have business with these gentlemen—I—I
Will forthwith join you.

Pauline. Do not tarry long! [*Exit into House*, L. S. E.

.

42. *Enter* BEAUSEANT *and* GLAVIS *from House*, L. S. E.

Melnotte. Release me from my oath,—I will not marry
    her!

Beauseant. Then thou art perjured.

Melnotte. No, I was not in my senses when I swore to
thee to marry her! I was blind to all but her scorn!—

deaf to all but my passion" and my rage"! Give me [54]
back my poverty and my honor !

Beauseant. It is too late,—you must * marry her ! and
this day ! I have a story already coined,—and sure to
pass current. This Damas suspects thee[5], he will set *
the police" to work ; thou wilt be detected—Pauline will
despise and execrate thee. Thou wilt be sent to the common gaol as a swindler.

43. *Melnotte.* Fiend !

Beauseant. And in the heat of the girl's[5] resentment
(you know of what resentment is capable) and the parents'[5]
shame, she will be induced * to marry the first that * offers
—even perhaps your humble' servant.*

Melnotte. You ! No ! that were worse—for thou hast no
mercy ! I will marry her—I will keep my oath. Quick, *
then, with the damnable invention ‡ thou art hatching;
—quick, if thou wouldst not have * me strangle thee or
myself.

Glavis. What * a tiger ! Too fierce for a Prince ; he
ought to have been the Grand' Turk.

Beauseant. Enough—I will despatch ; be prepared.

[*Exeunt* BEAUSEANT *and* GLAVIS *into House,* L. S. E.

44. *Enter* DAMAS, *from the House,* L. S. E., *with two
swords.*

Damas. Now, then, sir, the ladies are no longer * your
excuse. * I have brought you a couple of dictionaries;
let us see if your Highness can find out the Latin' for
bilbo.

Melnotte. Away, Sir !—I am * in no humor for jesting.

Damas. I see ‡ you understand something of the grammar; you decline the noun substantive "small sword"
with great ease; but that won't do *—you must take a
lesson in * *parsing.*

Melnotte. Fool!

Damas. Sir, a man who calls me a fool insults the lady who bore* me; there's no escape* for you— fight you shall, or——

✝ *Melnotte.* (L.) Oh, enough, enough!—take your ground.

45. (*They fight;* DAMAS *is disarmed.*—MELNOTTE *takes up the sword and returns it to* DAMAS *respectfully.*) A just punishment to the brave' soldier who robs the state of its best property—the sole* right to his valor and his life!

Damas. (R.) Sir, you fence exceedingly well; you must* be a man of honor—I don't care* a jot whether you are a prince'; but a man who has carte and tierce at his fingers'⁵ ends must be a gentleman.*

Melnotte (*aside*). Gentleman! Ay, I was a gentleman before I turned conspirator; for honest men are the gentlemen of Nature! Colonel, they tell me‡ you rose from the ranks.

Damas. I did.

Melnotte. And in two years?

46. *Damas.* It is* true; that's no wonder in our army at present. Why, the oldest general' in the service' is* scarcely thirty, and we have some of two-and-twenty.

Melnotte. Two-and-twenty?

Damas. Yes; in the French army, nowadays, promotion is not a matter of purchase. We are all heroes, because we may all be generals. We have no fear of the cypress, because we may all hope for the laurel.

Melnotte. A general' at two-and-twenty (*turning away*) —Sir, I may ask you a favor one of these days.

Damas. Sir, I shall be proud to grant it. It is astonishing how much I like a man after I've fought with him.

[‡ *Hides the swords,* R.

47. *Enter* Madame *and* Beauseant *from House*, L. S. E.

Madame Deschap. Oh, Prince'!—Prince!—What do I hear? You must* fly,—you must quit us!

Melnotte. I!

Beauseant. Yes, Prince; read this letter, just* received from my friend at Paris, one of the Directory;[3] they are very suspicious of princes, and your family[3] take* part with the Austrians. Knowing that I introduced your Highness at Lyons, my friend writes to me to say that you must quit the town immediately, or ‡ you will be arrested,—thrown into prison'',—perhaps guillotined! Fly! I will order* horses to your carriage instantly. Fly to Marseilles; there you can take ship* to Leghorn.

Madame Deschap. And what's to become of Pauline? Am * I not to be a mother to a princess, after all?

48. *Enter* Pauline *and* M. Deschappelles *from House*, L. S. E.

Pauline (throwing herself into Melnotte's[5] arms). You must * leave us!—Leave Pauline!

Beauseant. Not* a moment is to be wasted.

Mons. Deschap. I will go to the magistrates and inquire—

Beauseant. Then he is lost; the magistrates, hearing ‡ he is suspected, will order his* arrest.

Madame Deschap. And shall I not be Princess Dowager?

Beauseant. Why* not? There* is only one thing to be done:—send for the priest—let * the marriage take place* at once, and the Prince carry home a bride!

Melnotte. Impossible!—(*Aside.*) Villain!—I know not what I say.

Madame Deschap. What! lose my child?

Beauseant. And gain a Princess !

49. *Madame Deschap.* Oh, Monsieur Beauseant, you are so very* kind,—it must be so,*—we ought* not to be selfish,—my daughter's⁵ happiness is at stake.* She will go away, too,* in a coach and six !

Pauline. Thou art here still,—I cannot part from thee, —my heart will break.

Melnotte. But thou wilt not consent to this hasty union, —thou wilt not wed an outcast,—a fugitive.

Pauline. Ah ! If thou art in danger, who should* share it but Pauline ?

Melnotte (aside). Distraction !—if the earth could* swallow me !

Mons. Deschap. Gently !—gently ! The settlements— the contracts—my daughter's⁵ dowry !

50. *Melnotte.* The dowry !—I am not base enough for that ; no, not one farthing !

Beauseant (to MADAME). Noble' fellow ! Really, your good husband is too mercantile in these matters. Monsieur' Deschappelles, you hear his Highness ; we can arrange the settlements by proxy,—'tis the way* with people of quality.

Mons. Deschap. But—

Madame Deschap. Hold your tongue !—Don't expose yourself !

Beauseant. I will bring the priest in a trice. Go in, all of you, and prepare : the carriage shall be at the door before the ceremony is over.

Madame Deschap. Be sure* ‡ there are six horses, Beauseant ! You are very good to have forgiven us for⁶ refusing you ; but, you see—a prince !

51. *Beauseant.* And such* a prince ! Madame, I cannot blush at the success of so* illustrious a rival.—(*Aside.*) Now will I follow them to the village'—enjoy my triumph, and to-morrow—in the hour of thy shame and grief,[4] I think, proud girl,‡ thou wilt prefer even these arms to those of the' gardener's [5] son.   [*Exit* BEAUSEANT.

Madame Deschap. Come, Monsieur Deschappelles— give your arm to her Highness that is to be.*

Mons. Deschap. I don't like * doing business in such a hurry—'tis not the way* with the house of Deschappelles & Co.

Madame Deschap. There, now—you fancy you are in the counting-house, don't[6] you?

                 ‡[*Pushes him to* PAULINE.

52. *Melnotte.* Stay,—stay, Pauline—one word. Have you no scruple—no fear? Speak—it is* not yet too late.

Pauline. When I loved thee, thy fate became mine.— Triumph or danger—joy or sorrow—I am by thy side.*

Damas. Well, well, Prince, thou art a lucky man to be so loved. She is* a good little girl, in spite of her foibles—make her as happy as if she were* not to be a princess (*slapping him on the shoulder*). Come, Sir, I wish* you joy—young—tender—lovely; zounds, I envy you!

Melnotte (who has stood apart in gloomy abstraction). DO YOU?*[6]

53. * On the stage the following lines are added:

> Do you? Wise judges are we of each other.
> " Woo, wed, and bear her home!" so runs the bond .
> To which I sold[7] myself—and then—what then?
> Away!—I will not look beyond the hour.*
> Like children in the dark, I dare not face
> The shades that * gather round me in the distance.
> You envy me—I thank you—you may read
> My joy upon my brow—I thank you, Sir!
> If hearts had audible language, you would hear
> How mine would answer when you talk of ENVY.

PICTURE.—END OF ACT II.

ACT III.

54. SCENE I.—*The Exterior of the Golden Lion—time, twilight. The moon rises during the Scene.*

Enter LANDLORD *and his* DAUGHTER, *from the Inn,* L. D. F.

Landlord. Ha! ha! ha! Well, I never shall get* over it. Our Claude is a prince with a vengeance now. His carriage breaks down at my inn—ha! ha!

Janet. And what airs the young lady gives herself! "Is this* the best room‡ you have,⁸⁶ young woman?" with such a toss* of the head!

Landlord. Well, get in, Janet, get in and see* to the supper; the servants must sup before they go back.

[*Exeunt* LANDLORD *and* JANET, L. D. F.

Enter BEAUSEANT *and* GLAVIS, R.

Beauseant. You see our Princess is lodged at last—one stage more, and she'll be at her journey's⁵⁵ end—the beautiful palace at the foot of the Alps!—ha! ha!

55. *Glavis.* Faith, I pity the poor Pauline—especially if she's going to sup at the Golden⁵⁵ Lion (*makes a wry face*). I shall never forget that cursed ragout'.

Enter MELNOTTE *from the Inn,* L. D. F.

Beauseant. Your servant, my Prince'; you reigned⁷ most worthily. I condole with you on your abdication. I am afraid that your Highness's⁵ retinue are³¹ not very faithful servants. I think‡ they will quit you at the moment of your fall—'tis the fate of greatness.² But

C*

you are welcome * to your fine clothes—also the diamond ⁵⁵ snuff-box, which Louis XIV. gave to your great-
great-grandmother.

Glavis. And the ring with which your grandfather, the
Doge of Venice, married the Adriatic.

56. *Melnotte.* Have I kept my oath, gentlemen? Say
—have I kept my oath?

Beauseant. Most religiously.

Melnotte. Then you have done * with me and mine—
away with you!

Beauseant. How, knave?

Melnotte. Look you, our bond is over. Proud con-
querors that we are, we have won the victory over a
simple girl—compromised her honor—embittered her life
—blasted, in their very * blossoms, all the flowers of her
youth. This* is your triumph,—it is my shame! (‡ *Turns
to* BEAUSEANT.) Enjoy that triumph, but not in my sight.
I *was* her betrayer—I *am* her protector! Cross * but her
path—one word of scorn, one look of insult—nay, but
one quiver of that mocking ⁵¹ lip, and I will teach thee
that bitter word thou hast graven eternally in this heart
—*Repentance!*

57. *Beauseant.* His Highness is most grandiloquent.

Melnotte. Highness* me no more! Beware! Remorse
has made * me a new being. Away with you! There is
danger ' in me. Away!

Glavis (aside). He's an awkward * fellow to deal with;
come away, Beauseant.

Beauseant. I know the respect ' due to rank. Adieu ',
my Prince '. Any commands at Lyons? Yet hold—I
promised you two hundred louis on * your wedding-day;
here * they are.

Melnotte (dashing the purse to the ground). I gave you

revenge, I did not sell it. Take up your silver, Judas ' ;
take it. Ay, it is fit you should learn to stoop.

Beauseant. You will beg my pardon * for this some
day. (*Aside to* GLAVIS.) Come to my chateau—I shall
return hither to-morrow, to * learn how Pauline likes her
new dignity.

58. *Melnotte.* Are you not gone yet?

Beauseant. Your Highness's⁵ most obedient, most faithful—

Glavis. And most humble servants. Ha ! ha !

[*Exeunt* BEAUSEANT *and* GLAVIS, R.

Melnotte. Thank Heaven, I had no weapon, or I should
have slain them. Wretch ! what can I say? where turn ?
On all sides mockery—the very * boors within—(*Laughter
from the Inn*)—'Sdeath, if even in this short absence "
the exposure should have * chanced ! I will call her.
We will go hence. I have already sent one * ‡ I can trust
to my mother's⁵ house; there, at least, none can insult
her agony—gloat upon her shame ! There alone must
she learn what * a villain she has sworn to love. [*As he
turns to the door,*

Enter PAULINE *from the Inn*, L. D. F.

59. *Pauline.* Ah, my Lord, what a place ! I never
saw such * rude people. They stare and wink so. I think
the very * sight of a prince', though he travels incognito,
turns their honest heads. What * a pity the carriage
should break down in such a spot !—you are not well—
the drops * stand on your brow—your hand is feverish.

Melnotte. Nay, it is but a passing spasm; * the air'—

Pauline. Is not the soft air ' of your native south.

[*Pause.* *

How pale ' he is—indeed thou art not well.
Where are our people ? * I will call them.

Melnotte. Hold !
I—I am well.
    60. *Pauline.* Thou art !—Ah ! now I know it.
Thou fanciest, my kind Lord—I know * thou * dost—
Thou fanciest ‡ these rude walls,* these rustic gossips,
Brick'd floors, sour wine, coarse viands, vex Pauline ;
And so they might,⁶¹ but thou art by * my side,
And I forget all else ! *

Enter LANDLORD, *from* D. F., *the servants peeping and
    laughing over * his shoulder.*

  Landlord. My Lord—your Highness—
Will your most noble ' Excellency choose—
    Melnotte. Begone, Sir ! [*Exit* LANDLORD, *laughing.*
    Pauline. How could * they have learn'd thy rank ?
One's * servants are so vain !—nay, let * it not
Chafe thee, sweet Prince !—a few short days, and we
Shall see thy palace by its lake of silver,
And—nay, nay, spendthrift, is thy wealth of smiles
Already drain'd, or dost thou play the miser ?
    61. *Melnotte.* Thine eyes would call up smiles in
        deserts, fair one ! *
Let us escape these rustics. Close * at hand
There is a cot, where I have bid prepare
Our evening lodgment—a rude, homely roof,
But honest, where our welcome * will not be
Made * torture by the vulgar eyes and tongues ⁴³
That are as death to Love ! A heavenly night !
The wooing air ' and the soft moon invite us.
Wilt walk ? I pray thee, now,—I know the path,
Ay, every inch* of it !
    62. *Pauline.* What, *thou !* methought ‡
Thou wert a stranger in these parts. Ah ! truant,

Some village [5] beauty lured thee ;—thou art now
Grown * constant.

Melnotte. Trust me.

Pauline. Princes [21] are so changeful !

Melnotte. Come, dearest, come.

Pauline. Shall I not call our people
To light us ?

Melnotte. Heaven will lend its stars for torches !
It is not far.

Pauline. The night [5] breeze chills me.

Melnotte. Nay,
Let me thus mantle thee ;—it is * not cold.

Pauline. Never beneath thy smile !

Melnotte (aside). Oh, Heaven ! forgive me ! [*Exeunt,* R.

63. SCENE II.—MELNOTTE'S *cottage*—WIDOW *bustling* *
about—A table spread * *for supper.*

Widow. So! I think that looks * very neat. He sent
me a line so blotted that I can scarcely read it, to say ‡ he
·vould * be here almost immediately. She must * have
loved him well indeed, to have forgotten his birth: for
though he was introduced to her in disguise, he is too
honorable * not to have revealed to her the artifice '
which her love only could forgive. Well, I do not
wonder at it; for though my son is not a * prince ', he
ought * to be one, and that's * almost as good. [*Knock* *
at the D. *in* F.] Ah! here* they are.

Enter MELNOTTE *and* PAULINE, *from* D. *in* F.

64. *Widow.* Oh, my boy, the pride of my heart!—
welcome, welcome ! I beg pardon, Ma'am, but I do love
him so ! *

Pauline. Good woman, I really—Why, Prince, what is

this?—does the old woman know you? Oh, I guess *
you have done ‡ her some service: * another proof of
your kind heart, is⁶ it not?

Melnotte. Of my kind heart, ay.

Pauline. So, you know the Prince'?

Widow. Know him, Madame?—ah, I begin to fear ‡ it
is you who know him not !

Pauline. Do you think‡ she is mad? Can we stay
here, my Lord? I think‡ there's something very wild
about * her.

65. *Melnotte.* Madame, I—No, I cannot tell ‡ her !
My knees knock* together: what * a coward is a man who
has lost his honor ! Speak to her—speak to her—(*to his
mother*)—tell her that—oh, Heaven, that* I were dead !

Pauline. How* confused he looks!—this strange place "
—this woman—what can it mean? I half suspect—Who
are you, Madame?—who are you? can't * you speak? are
you struck dumb? *

Widow. Claude, you have not deceived her?—ah,
shame upon you! I thought that before you went to the
altar she was * to have known all?

Pauline. All! what? My blood freezes* in my veins!

Widow. Poor lady !—Dare I tell ‡ her, Claude?

[MELNOTTE *makes a sign of assent.*

66. Know you not then, Madame, that this young
man is of poor though honest parents? Know you not
that you are wedded to my son, Claude Melnotte?

Pauline. Your son ! hold ! hold ! do not speak to me—
(‡ *approaches* MELNOTTE *and lays her hand on his arm.*) Is
this a jest? Is* it? I know it is⁶¹: only speak—one
word—one look—one smile. I cannot believe—I,* who
loved thee so—I cannot believe that thou art such a——
No, I will not wrong thee by a harsh* word ; speak !

Melnotte. Leave us; have pity* on her—on me: leave us.

Wi.low. Oh, Claude! that* I should* live to see thee
bowed by shame! thee, of whom I was so proud!

> [*Exit* Widow, *by the staircase*, R. U. E.

67. *Pauline.* Her son! her son!
Melnotte. Now, lady, hear me.
Pauline. Hear thee!
Ay, speak. Her son! have fiends a parent? speak,
That* thou may'st silence curses. Speak!
Melnotte. No, curse me:
Thy curse would blast me less than thy forgiveness.
Pauline (laughing wildly*). "This* is thy palace, where
the perfumed light
Steals* through the mists of alabaster lamps,
And every air is heavy with the sighs
Of orange* groves, and music from sweet lutes,
And murmurs of low fountains, that gush forth
I' the midst of roses"! Dost thou like the picture?"*
68. *This** is my bridal home, and *thou* my bridegroom!
O fool! O dupe! O wretch! I see* it all—
The by-word and the jeer* of every tongue   ·
In Lyons! Hast thou in thy heart one touch*
Of human kindness? if thou hast, why, kill me,
And save thy wife from madness. No, it cannot,*
It cannot be! this* is some horrid dream:
I shall wake soon *(touching him).* Art flesh? art man? or but
The shadows seen[9] in sleep? It is too* real.
What have I done to thee? how sinn'd* against thee,
That thou shouldst* crush me thus?
69. *Melnotte.* Pauline! by pride,[21]
Angels[2] have fallen ere thy time; by pride,
That sole alloy of thy most lovely mould*—
The evil spirit* of a bitter love,
And a revengeful heart, had power* upon thee.—
From* my first years, my soul was fill'd with thee:

I saw thee, midst the flowers the lowly boy
Tended, unmark'd by thee, a spirit* of bloom,
And joy⁴ and freshness,⁴ as if* spring² itself
Were made* a living thing, and wore thy shape!
70. I saw thee! and the passionate heart of man
Enter'd the breast of the wild-dreaming boy;
And from that hour I grew*—what to the last*
I shall be—thine adorer!* Well! this love,
Vain, frantic, guilty, if thou wilt, became
A fountain of ambition" and bright hope:
I thought of tales that by the winter⁵ hearth*
Old gossips tell—how* maidens, sprung from Kings,
Have stoop'd from their high sphere; how Love, like Death,
Levels all ranks, and lays the shepherd's⁵ crook
Beside the sceptre'. Thus* I made my home*
In the soft palace of a fairy* Future!
71. My father died; and I, the peasant-born,
Was my own* lord. Then* did I seek to rise*
Out of the prison" of my mean estate;
And, with such* jewels as the exploring* Mind
Brings* from the caves * of Knowledge, buy my ransom*
From those twin gaolers of the daring heart—
Low Birth and iron⁵ Fortune. Thy bright image",
Glass'd* in my soul, took all the hues* of glory,
And lured me on to those inspiring* toils
By which man masters men!
72. A midnight* student o'er the dreams of sages':
For thee I sought to borrow from each Grace",
And every Muse", such* attributes as lend
Ideal* charms to Love. I thought of thee,
And Passion²" taught me poesy²—of thee!
And on the painter's⁵ canvas grew the life
Of beauty²—Art' became the shadow
Of the dear starlight* of thy haunting eyes!

Men² called me vain, some mad*—I heeded not,
But still toil'd on, hoped on, for it was* sweet,
If not to win, to feel* more worthy thee!

73. *Pauline.* Has he a magic to exorcise hate?

Melnotte. At last, in one mad* hour, I dared to pour*
The thoughts that burst* their channels into song,
And sent them to thee—such* a tribute, lady,
As beauty² rarely scorns, even from the meanest.
The name—appended by the burning heart
That long'd* to show ‡ its idol what bright things
It had⁷ created—yea, the enthusiast's⁵ name,
That should* have been thy triumph, was⁷ thy scorn!
That very* hour—when passion ", turn'd to wrath,
Resembled hatred most; when thy disdain

74. Made* my whole soul a chaos² = in that hour
The tempters found⁷ me a revengeful tool
For their revenge! Thou hadst⁷ trampled on the worm—
It turn'd⁷ and stung thee!

Pauline. Love, Sir, hath no sting.
What was the slight of a poor powerless girl,
To* the deep wrong of this most vile revenge?
Oh, how I loved this man! a serf! a slave!

Melnotte. Hold, lady! No, not slave! Despair is free.*
I will not tell* thee of the throes, the struggles,
The anguish, the remorse. No, let it pass!
And let me come to such most poor atonement*
Yet* in my power. Pauline!

75.   [*Approaching her with great emotion, and
                        about to take her* hand.*

Pauline. No, touch me not!
I know my fate. You are, by* law, my tyrant;
And I—oh Heaven! a peasant's⁵ wife! I'll work,
Toil, drudge; do what thou wilt; but touch me not;
Let my wrongs* make me sacred!

Melnotte. Do not fear me. [54]
Thou dost not know me, Madame : at the altar
My vengeance ceased, my guilty oath expired !
Henceforth, no image of some marbled saint,
Niched * in cathedral's [5] aisles, is hallow'd * more
From the rude hand of sacrilegious wrong.

76. I am thy husband ; nay, thou need'st not shudder :
Here, at thy feet, I lay a husband's [5] rights.
A marriage thus unholy *—unfulfill'd—
A bond of fraud *—is, by the laws of France,
Made void * and null.   To-night, then, sleep—in peace.
To-morrow, pure and virgin as this morn
I bore thee, bathed in blushes, from the altar,
Thy father's [5] arms shall take * thee to thy home.
The law shall do thee justice ", and restore
Thy right to bless another with thy love.

77. And when * thou art happy, and ‡ hast half * forgot
Him * who so loved—so wrong'd thee, think at least
‡ Heaven left some remnant of the angel still
In that poor peasant's [5] nature !
Ho ! my mother !

       [WIDOW [2] *comes down stairs*, R. U. E.
Conduct this lady—(she is not my wife ;
She is our guest, our honor'd guest, my mother !)
To the poor chamber where the sleep of virtue [5]
Never beneath my father's [5] honest roof
E'en villains dared to mar !   Now, lady, now,
I think ‡ thou wilt believe me.—Go, my mother.

  Widow. She is not thy wife !

  Melnotte. Hush ! hush ! for mercy * sake
Speak not, but go.   [WIDOW *ascends the stairs*, R. U. E.
(*Melnotte, sinking down.*) All angels bless and guard her !

       PICTURE.—END OF ACT III.

ACT IV.

78. SCENE I.—*The Cottage as before*—MELNOTTE *seated before a table—writing* implements, etc.—(Day break-ing.*)*

Melnotte. Hush, hush!—she sleeps at last!—thank * Heaven, for awhile she forgets even that I live! Her sobs, which have gone to my heart the whole, long, deso-late night, have ceased!—all calm—all still! I will * go now; I will send this letter to Pauline's[5] father—when * he arrives, I will place in his hands my own* consent to the[14] divorce'; and then, O France! my country! accept among thy protectors, thy defenders—the Peas-ant's Son! Our country is less proud than custom, and does not refuse the blood, the heart, the right hand of the poor man!

WIDOW[23] *comes down stairs,* R. U. E.

79. *Widow.* My son, thou hast acted ill, but sin[21] brings its own * punishment. In * the hour of thy re-morse, it is * not for a mother to reproach * thee.

Melnotte. What * is past is past. There is a future left to all men who have the virtue to repent and the energy to atone.* Thou shalt be proud of thy son, yet; mean-while, remember ‡ this poor lady has been grievously injured. For the sake* of thy son's[5] conscience", re-spect, honor, bear * with her. If she weep, console; if she chide, be silent! 'Tis but a little while more; I shall send an express fast as horse can speed to her father. Farewell! I shall return shortly.

80. *Widow.* It is the only course left * to thee: thou wert led astray,* but thou art not hardened. Thy heart is right still, as ever it was, when, in thy most ambitious hopes, thou wert never ashamed * of thy poor mother!

Melnotte. Ashamed of thee! No, if I yet endure, yet live, yet hope, it is only because I would not die till I have redeemed the noble' heritage' I have lost—the heritage I took unstained from thee and my dead father —a proud conscience" and an honest* name. I shall win them back yet; Heaven bless you! [*Exit,* D. *in* F.

Widow. My dear Claude! how my heart bleeds for him!

[PAULINE *looks down from above, and, after a pause, descends.*

81. *Pauline.* Not here! he spares me that pain at least; so far he is considerate—yet the place seems still more desolate without him. Oh that * I could hate him, the gardener's ⁵ son! and yet how nobly he—no—no— no, I will not be so * mean a thing as to forgive him!

Widow. Good-morning, Madame; I would have waited on you if I had known ‡ you were stirring.

Pauline. It is no matter, * Ma'am; your son's ⁵ wife ought * to wait on herself.

Widow. My son's wife; let not that thought vex you, Madame—he tells me that you will have your divorce'. And I hope ‡ I shall live to see him smile again. **82.** There * are maidens in this village', young and fair, Madame, who may yet console him.

Pauline. I dare say—they are very welcome; and when the divorce' is got, he will marry again. I am sure * I hope so.   [*Weeps.*

Widow. He could* have married the richest girl in* the province ", if he had pleased * it; but his head was turned,* poor child! he could think* of nothing but you.   [*Weeps.*

Pauline. Don't weep, *mother !*

Widow. Ah, he has behaved very ill, I know; but love is so headstrong in the young. Don't weep, Madame.

Pauline. So, as you were saying ;* go on.

Widow. Oh, I cannot excuse him, Ma'am ; he was not in his right senses.*

83. *Pauline.* But he always—always (*sobbing*) loved —loved me,⁵ then ?

Widow. He thought * of nothing else ; see here—he learned to paint that he might take your likeness (‡*uncovers the picture*). But that's all over* now ; I trust you have cured him⁵ of his folly. But, dear heart, you have had no * breakfast !

Pauline. I can't take anything—don't trouble yourself.

Widow. Nay, Madame, be persuaded : a little coffee will refresh you. Our milk and eggs are excellent '. I will get out Claude's⁵ coffee-cup—it is of real Sevre ;* he saved up all his money to buy it⁵ three years ago,* because the name of *Pauline* was inscribed * on it.

84. *Pauline.* Three years ago ! Poor Claude ! Thank you, I think ‡ I will have some coffee. Oh, if* he were but* a poor gentleman, even a merchant ; but a gardener's⁵ son ! and what * a home ! Oh, no, it is too* dreadful ! [*They seat themselves at the table*—BEAUSEANT *opens the lattice and looks in* F.

Beauseant. So—so—the coast * is clear ! I saw⁷³ Claude in the lane ; I shall have an excellent ' opportunity.

[*Shuts the lattice and knocks at the* D. *in* F.

Pauline (starting). Can it be my father ? He has not sent for him yet ? No, he cannot be in such a hurry to get rid of me.

Widow. It is not time for your father to arrive yet ; it must be * some neighbor.

Pauline. Don't admit any* one. [WIDOW *opens the*
D. *in* F.

85. BEAUSEANT *pushes her aside and enters.*

Ah! Heavens! that hateful Beauseant! This is indeed
bitter.

Beauseant. Good morning, Madame! Oh, Widow,[23]
your son begs* you will have the goodness to go to him
in the village '—he wants to speak to you on particular
business: you'll find him at* the inn, or the grocer's[5]
shop, or the baker's, or at* some other friend's of your
family—make haste!

Pauline. Don't leave me, mother! don't leave me!

Beauseant (with great respect). Be not alarmed, Madame.
Believe me your friend, your servant.*

Pauline. Sir, I have no fear of you, even in this house!
Go, Madame, if your son wishes it; I will not contradict .
his commands whilst at least he has still the right to be
obeye l.

Widow. I don't understand this; however, I shan't be
long gone.   [*Exit* D. *in* F.

86. *Pauline.* Sir, I divine the object of your visit—
you wish to exult in the humiliation" of one* who humbled you. Be it so;* I am prepared to endure all—even
your presence"!

Beauseant. You mistake* me, Madame—Pauline, you
mistake* me! I come* to lay my fortune" at your feet.
You must already be disenchanted with this impostor;
these walls are not worthy to be hallowed by your beauty!
Beloved, beautiful Pauline! fly with me*—my carriage
waits without*—I will bear* you to a home more meet*
for your reception. Wealth,[27] luxury, station—all shall
yet be yours.* I forget your past[5] disdain—I remember
only your bea ty and my unconquerable love!

87. *Pauline.* Sir, leave this house: it is humble', but a husband's⁵ roof, however * lowly, is, in the eyes of God and man, the temple' of a wife's honor! Know that I would rather * starve—yes! with him * who has betrayed me, than accept your lawful * hand, even were you the prince whose * name he bore! Go!

Beauseant. What, is not your pride humbled yet?

Pauline. Sir, what * was pride in prosperity, in affliction'' becomes virtue.

Beauseant. Look round: these rugged floors—these homely walls—this wretched struggle of poverty for comfort—think of this! * and contrast with such a picture the refinement, the luxury, the pomp that the wealthiest gentleman of Lyons offers to the loveliest lady. Ah, hear me!

88. *Pauline.* Oh! my father! why did I leave you? why am I thus friendless? Sir, you see before you a betrayed, injured, miserable woman! respect her anguish!

MELNOTTE *opens the* D. *in* F. *and silently pauses at the threshold.*

Beauseant. No! let me rather thus console it; let me snatch from those lips one breath * of that fragrance which should never be wasted on the low churl thy husband.

Pauline. Help! Claude! Claude! have I no protector?

Beauseant. Be silent! (*showing a pistol.*) See, I do not come unprepared * even for violence''. I will brave all things—thy husband and all his race—for thy sake.* Thus, then, I clasp thee!⁵

89. *Melnotte* (*dashing him to the other end of the stage*). Pauline—look up, Pauline! thou art safe. *

Beauseant (*levelling his pistol*). Dare you thus insult a man of my birth, ruffian?

Pauline. Oh, spare him—spare my husband! Beauseant—Claude—no—no!   [*Faints.*

Melnotte. Miserable' trickster! shame upon you! brave
devices to terrify a woman! coward—you tremble—you
have outraged the laws—you know that your weapon is
harmless—you have the courage' of the mountebank, not
the bravo! Pauline, there * is no danger'.

Beauseant. I wish thou wert a gentleman—as it is, thou
art beneath me. Good-day, and a happy honey-moon.
(*Aside.*) I will not die till I am avenged.

        [*Exit* BEAUSEANT, D. *in* F.

90. *Melnotte.* I hold her in these arms—the last em-
    brace!

Never, ah, never more shall this dear head
Be pillow'd * on the heart that should * have shelter'd
And has betray'd! Soft!—soft! one kiss—poor wretch!*
No scorn on that pale' lip forbids me now!
One kiss—so* ends all record of my crime!
It is the seal upon the tomb of Hope,
By which, like some lost,⁵ sorrowing angel, sits
Sad Memory² evermore. She breathes—she moves*—
She wakes to scorn,* to hate, but not to shudder
Beneath the touch of my abhorréd love.

        [‡ *Places her on a seat.*

There—we are strangers* now!

91. *Pauline.* All gone—all calm—
Is *every* thing a dream? thou art safe, unhurt—
I do not love thee; but—but—I am a woman,*
And—and—no blood is spilt?

Melnotte. No, lady, no;
My guilt has not deserved so * rich a blessing
As even danger' in thy cause''.

Enter WIDOW,[2] *from* D. *in* F.

Widow. My son, I have been everywhere in * search
of you ; why did [73] you send * for me?

Melnotte. I did not send * for you.

Widow. No? but I must * tell you ‡ your express has
returned.

Melnotte. So soon! impossible!'

92. *Widow.* Yes: he met the lady's [5] mother and
father on * the road ; they were going [73] into the country
on * a visit. Your messenger says that Monsieur Deschappelles turned * almost white with anger, when he
read [73] your letter. They will be here almost immediately.
Oh, Claude, Claude! what will they do to you? How * I
tremble! Ah, Madame! do not let them injure him—
if you knew how he doted on you!

Pauline. Injure him! no, Ma'am, be not afraid;*—
My father! how shall I meet him? how go back * to
Lyons? the scoff of the whole city! Cruel', cruel
Claude! (*In great agitation.*) Sir, you have acted most
treacherously!

Melnotte. I know it, Madame.

93. *Pauline (aside).* If he would * but ask me to
forgive him! [5]—I never can forgive you, Sir!

Melnotte. I never dared to hope it.

Pauline. But you are my husband now, and I have
sworn to—to love you, Sir.

Melnotte. That * was under a false belief, Madame;
Heaven and the laws will release you from your vow.

Pauline. He will drive * me mad! If he were but *
less proud—if he would * but ask me to remain—hark,
hark! I hear the wheels of the carriage—Sir—Claude,
they are [71] coming; have you no word to say ere it is too
late—Quick—speak!

D   7

Melnotte. I can only congratulate you on your release. Behold * your parents ' !

94. *Enter* MONSIEUR *and* MADAME DESCHAPPELLES *and* COLONEL [23] DAMAS, D. *in* F.

Mons. Deschap. My child !—my child !

Madame Deschap. Oh, my poor Pauline !—what * a villainous hovel this is ! Old * woman, get me a chair— I shall faint—I certainly shall.[62] What will the world say? Child, you have been a fool. A mother's [5] heart is easily broken.[9]

Damas. Ha, ha !—most noble ' Prince '—I am sorry to see a man of your quality in such a condition ; I am afraid * your Highness will go to the House of Correction ".

Melnotte. Taunt on, Sir—I spared *you* when you were unarmed—I am unarmed now. A man who has no excuse " for crime ' is indeed defenceless !

Damas. There's * something fine in the rascal, after all !

95. *Mons. Deschap.* Where is the impostor? Are you thus shameless, traitor? Can you brave the presence " of that girl's [5] father?

Melnotte. Strike me, if it please * you—you *are* her father !

Pauline. Sir—sir, for my sake ; *—whatever his guilt, he has acted nobly in atonement.

Madame Deschap. Nobly ! Are you mad, girl ? I have no patience * with you—to disgrace all your family thus ! Nobly ! Oh, you abominable', hardened, pitiful, mean, ugly villain !

Damas. Ugly ! Why, he was beautiful, yesterday.

Pauline. Madame, this * is his roof, and he * is my husband. Respect your daughter, and let blame fall alone on her.

Madame Deschap. You—you—oh, I'm choking!

Mons. Deschap. Sir, it were idle* to waste reproach upon a conscience" like yours—**96.**═You renounce all pretensions to the person of this lady?

Melnotte. I do.⁶² (*Gives a paper.*) Here* is my consent to a divorce'—my full confession of the fraud, which annuls marriage. Your daughter has been foully wronged —I grant it, Sir; but her own* lips will tell you, that from the hour in which she crossed this threshold, I returned to my own* station, and respected hers. Pure and inviolate as when yester morn you laid⁷³ your hand upon her head and blessed her,⁵ I yield her back* to you. For myself—I deliver you forever from my presence". An outcast and a criminal, I seek some distant land, where I may* mourn my sin, and pray for your daughter's⁵ peace. Farewell—farewell to you all forever!

97. *Widow.* Claude, Claude, you will* not leave your poor mother? *She* does not disown you⁵ in your sorrow —no, not even in your guilt. No divorce' can separate a mother from her son.

Pauline. This poor widow teaches me⁵ my duty. No, mother,* no—for you are now *my* mother also!—nor should* any law, human or divine, separate the wife from her husband's⁵ sorrows. Claude, Claude—all is forgotten —forgiven—I am thine* forever!*

Madame Deschap. What do I hear?—Come away, or never see my face* again.

Mons. Deschap. Pauline, *we* never betrayed⁷³ you!— will* you forsake us⁵ for him?

Pauline (*going back* to her father*). Oh, no! but you will forgive him, too; we will live together—he shall be your son.

98. *Mons. Deschap.* Never! Cling to him and forsake your parents'! His home shall be yours*—his fortune

yours—his fate yours : the wealth ‡ I have acquired by
honest industry shall never enrich the dishonest man.

Pauline. And you would have* a wife enjoy luxury
while a husband toils!   Claude, take me;⁵⁴ thou canst
not give me wealth, ²⁷ titles, station—but thou canst give
me a true heart.   I will work for thee, tend thee, bear*
with thee, and never, never shall these lips reproach thee
for the past.

Damas. I'll be hanged if I am not going to blubber !

99. *Melnotte.* This is the heaviest* blow of all !—
What* a heart I have wronged !   Do not fear me,⁵⁴ Sir ;
I àm not at all hardened—I will not rob her of a holier
love than mine.   Pauline ! angel of love and mercy ! your
memory shall lead me back to virtue !   The husband of a
being so beautiful in her noble' and sublime' tenderness
may* be poor—may be low-born—(there is no guilt* in
the decrees of Providence !)—but he should* be one* who
can look thee in the face without* a blush,—to whom thy
love does not bring remorse,—who can fold thee to his
ʳeart and say,—"*Here** there is no deceit !"——I am
not that man !

100. *Damas (aside to* MELNOTTE). Thou art a noble'
fellow, notwithstanding,* and wouldst make an excellent
soldier.   Serve in my regiment.   I have had a letter from
the Directory—our young General' takes the command of
the army in* Italy ; I am to join⁵ him at Marseilles—I
will depart this day if thou wilt go with me.

Melnotte. It is* the favor I would have asked* thee,
if* I had dared.   Place me wherever a foe is most
dreaded, *—wherever France most needs a life !

Damas. There shall not be a forlorn* hope without*
thee !

Melnotte. There* is my hand !   Mother ! your blessing.

ı01. I shall see you again,—a better man than a prince',

—a man who has bought the right to high thoughts by brave' deeds. And thou! thou! so wildly worshipped, so guiltily betrayed,—all is not yet lost!—for thy memory, at least, must be mine till* death! If I live, the name of him* ‡ thou hast once loved shall not rest dishonored; if I fall, amidst the carnage and the roar of battle, my soul will fly back * to thee, and Love shall share with Death my last sigh! More—more would I speak to thee!—to pray!—to bless! But, no!—when * I am less unworthy I will utter it⁵ to Heaven!—I cannot trust myself to——(*turning to* DESCHAPPELLES). Your pardon, Sir:—they are * my last words—Farewell! [*Exit*, D *in* F.

PICTURE.—END OF ACT IV.

ACT V.

SCENE I.—*The Streets of Lyons.*

(TWO YEARS AND A HALF FROM THE DATE OF ACT IV.)

Enter First, Second, and Third OFFICERS, L.

Enter DAMAS, *as a General,* L.

102. *Damas.* Good-morrow, gentlemen; I hope you will amuse yourselves during our short stay in Lyons. It is a fine city; improved since I left it. Ah! it is a pleasure to grow old,—when the years that bring decay to ourselves do but ripen the prosperity of our country. You have not met with Morier?

First Officer. No; we were just speaking of him.

Second Officer. Pray, General, can't you tell us who this Morier really is?

Damas. Is?—why, a Colonel in the French army.

Third Officer. True.   But what was he at first?

Damas. At first?—Why, a baby in long clothes, I suppose.

First Officer. Ha! ha!—Ever facetious, General!

Second Officer (to Third). The General is sore upon this point; you will only chafe him.—Any commands, General?

Damas. None.—Good-day to you!

[*Exeunt Second and Third Officers,* R.

103. *Damas.* Our comrades are very inquisitive.   Poor Morier is the subject of a vast deal of curiosity.

First Officer. Say interest, rather, General.   His constant melancholy,—the loneliness of his habits,—his daring valor,—his brilliant rise in the profession,—your friendship, and the favors of the Commander-in-Chief,—all tend to make him as much the matter of gossip as of admiration.   But where is he, General?   I have missed him all the morning.

Damas. Why, Captain, I'll let you into a secret.   My young friend has come with me to Lyons, in hopes of finding a miracle.

First Officer. A miracle!—

Damas. Yes, a miracle!   In other words,—a constant woman.

104. *First Officer.* Oh!—an affair of love!

Damas. Exactly so.   No sooner did he enter Lyons than he waved his hand to me, threw himself from his horse, and is now, I warrant, asking every one who can know anything about the matter whether a certain lady is still true to a certain gentleman!

. *First Officer.* Success to him!—and of that success there can be no doubt.   The gallant Colonel Morier, the hero of Lodi, might make his choice out of the proudest families in France.

Damas. Oh, if pride be a recommendation, the lady and her mother are most handsomely endowed. By the way, Captain, if you should chance to meet with Morier, tell him he will find me at the hotel.

First Officer. I will, General. [*Exit*, R.

105. *Damas.* Now will I go to the Deschappelles, and make a report to my young Colonel. Ha! by Mars, Bacchus, Apollo—here comes Monsieur Beauseant!

Enter BEAUSEANT, R.

Good-morrow, Monsieur Beauseant! How fares it with you?

Beauseant. (*Aside.*) Damas! that is unfortunate;—if the Italian campaign should have filled his pockets, he may seek to baffle me in the moment of my victory. (*Aloud.*) Your servant, General,—for such, I think, is your new distinction! Just arrived in Lyons?

Damas. Not an hour ago. Well, how go on the Deschappelles? Have they forgiven you in that affair of young Melnotte? You had some hand in that notable device,—eh?

106. *Beauseant.* Why, less than you think for! The fellow imposed upon me. I have set it all right now. What has become of him? He could not have joined the army, after all. There is no such name in the books.

Damas. I know nothing about Melnotte. As you say, I never heard the name in the Grand Army.

Beauseant. Hem!—you are not married, General?

Damas. Do I look like a married man, Sir?—No, thank Heaven! My profession is to make widows, not wives.

Beauseant. You must have gained much booty in Italy! Pauline will be your heiress—eh?

107. *Damas.* Booty! Not I! Heiress to what? Two trunks and a portmanteau,—four horses,—three swords,—

two suits of regimentals, and six pair of white leather in-expressibles!   A pretty fortune for a young lady!

Beauseant (aside). Then all is safe!   (*Aloud.*) Ha! ha! Is that really all your capital, General Damas? Why, I thought Italy had been a second Mexico to you soldiers.

Damas. All a toss-up, Sir.   I was not one of the lucky ones!   My friend Morier, indeed, saved something hand-some.   But our Commander-in-Chief took care of him, and Morier is a thrifty economical dog,—not like the rest of us soldiers, who spend our money carelessly as if it were our blood.

108. *Beauseant.* Well, it is no matter!   I do not want fortune with Pauline.   And you must know, General Damas, that your fair cousin has at length consented to reward my long and ardent attachment.

Damas. You! the devil! Why, she is already married. There is no divorce!

Beauseant. True; but this very day she is formally to authorize the necessary proceedings,—this very day she is to sign the contract that is to make her mine within one week from the day on which her present illegal marriage is annulled.

Damas. You tell me wonders!—Wonders! No; I be-lieve anything of women !

Beauseant. I must wish you good-morning.

[*As he is going,* L.,

Enter DESCHAPPELLES, R.

109. *Mons. Deschap.* Oh, Beauseant! well met.   Let us come to the notary at once.

Damas (to Deschappelles). Why, cousin?

Mons. Deschap. Damas, welcome to Lyons.   Pray call on us; my wife will be delighted to see you.

Damas. Your wife be——blessed for her condescension ! But (*taking him aside*) what do I hear? Is it possible that your daughter has consented to a divorce ?—that she will marry Monsieur Beauseant?

Mons. Deschap. Certainly ! what have you to say against it? A gentleman of birth, fortune, character. We are not so proud as we were ; even my wife has had enough of nobility and princes !

Damas. But Pauline loved that young man so tenderly.

110. *Mons. Deschap.* (*taking snuff.*) That was two years and a half ago !

Damas. Very true. Poor Melnotte !

Mons. Deschap. But do not talk of that impostor. I hope he is dead or has left the country. Nay, even were he in Lyons at this moment, he ought to rejoice that, in an honorable and suitable alliance, my daughter may forget her suffering and his crime.

Damas. Nay, if it be all settled I have no more to say. Monsieur Beauseant informs me that the contract is to be signed this very day.

Mons. Deschap. It is ; at one o'clock precisely. Will you be one of the witnesses?

Damas. I?—No ; that is to say—yes, certainly !—at one o'clock I will wait on you.

Mons. Deschap. Till then, adieu—come, Beauseant.

[*Exeunt* BEAUSEANT *and* DESCHAPPELLES, L.

111. *Damas.* The man who sets his heart upon a woman
Is a chameleon, and doth feed on air :
From air he takes his colors, holds his life,—
Changes with every wind,—grows lean or fat ;
Rosy with hope, or green with jealousy,
Or pallid with despair—just as the gale
Varies from north to south—from heat to cold !
Oh, woman ! woman ! thou shouldst have few sins
Of thine own to answer for ! Thou art the author

D*

Of such a book of follies in a man,
That it would need the tears of all the angels
To blot the record out !

112. *Enter* MELNOTTE, *pale and agitated*, R.

I need not tell thee !   Thou hast heard——
 Melnotte. The worst !
I have !
 Damas. Be cheered ; others are as fair as she is !
 Melnotte. Others !—the world is crumbled at my feet
She *was* my world; fill'd up the whole of being—
Smiled in the sunshine—walk'd the glorious earth—
Sate in my heart—was the sweet life of life :
The Past was hers; I dreamt not of a Future
That did not wear her shape !   Memory and Hope
Alike are gone.   Pauline is faithless !   Henceforth
The universal space is desolate !

113. *Damas.* Hope yet.
 Melnotte. Hope, yes !—one hope is left me still—
A soldier's grave !   Glory has died with Love !
I look into my heart, and where I saw
Pauline, see Death !
(*After a pause.*)   But am I not deceived?
I went but by the rumor of the town.
Rumor is false,—I was too hasty !   Damas
Whom hast thou seen?
 Damas. Thy rival and her father.
Arm thyself for the truth !   He heeds not——
 Melnotte. She
Will never know how deeply she was loved !

114. The charitable night, that wont to bring
Comfort to day, in bright and eloquent dreams,
Is henceforth leagued with misery !   Sleep, farewell,
Or else become eternal !   Oh, the waking

From false oblivion, and to see the sun,
And know she is another's !——

    Damas. Be a man !

    Melnotte. I am a man !—it is the sting of woe,
Like mine, that tells us we are men !

    Damas. The false one
Did not deserve thee.

    Melnotte. Hush !—no word against her !

115. Why should she keep, thro' years and silent absence,
The holy tablets of her virgin faith
True to a traitor's name ?　Oh, blame her not ;
It were a sharper grief to think her worthless
Than to be what I am !　To-day,—to-day !
They said " to-day !"　This day, so wildly welcomed—
This day, my soul had singled out of time
And mark'd for bliss !　This day ! oh, could I see her—
See her once more unknown ; but hear her voice,
So that one echo of its music might
Make ruin less appalling in its silence !

    116. *Damas.* Easily done !　Come with me to her house.
Your dress—your cloak—moustache—the bronzéd hue
Of time and toil—the name you bear—belief
In your absence, all will ward away suspicion.
Keep in the shade.　Ay, I would have you come.
There may be hope !　Pauline is yet so young,
They may have forced her to these second bridals
Out of mistaken love..

    Melnotte. No, bid me hope not !
Bid me not hope !　I could not bear again
To fall from such a heaven !　One gleam of sunshine,
And the ice breaks, and I am lost !　Oh, Damas,
There's no such thing as courage in a man ;
The veriest slave that ever crawl'd from danger
Might spurn me now.　**117.** When first I lost her, Damas,

I bore it, did I not? I still had hope,
And now I—I— [*Bursts into an agony of grief.*
    Damas. What, comrade! all the women
That ever smiled destruction on brave hearts,
Were not worth tears like these!
    Melnotte. 'Tis past—forget it.
I am prepared; life has no farther ills!
The cloud has broken in that stormy rain,
And on the waste I stand, alone with Heaven!
    Damas. His very face is changed! a breaking heart
Does its work soon!—Come, Melnotte, rouse thyself:
One effort more.   Again thou'lt see her.
    118. *Melnotte.* See her!
There is a passion in that simple sentence
That shivers all the pride and power of reason
Into a chaos!
    Damas. Time wanes;—come, ere yet
It be too late.
    Melnotte. Terrible words—"*Too late!*"
Lead on.   One last look more, and then——
    Damas. Forget her!
    Melnotte. Forget her, yes!—For death remembers not.
                                        [*Exeunt,* L.

SCENE II.—*A room in the house of* MONSIEUR DESCHAP-
    PELLES; PAULINE *seated, in great dejection.*

    Pauline. It is so, then.   I must be false to Love,
Or sacrifice a father!   Oh, my Claude,
My lover and my husband! have I lived
To pray that thou mayst find some fairer boon
Than the deep faith of this devoted heart,—
Nourish'd till now—now broken!

119. *Enter* Monsieur Deschappelles, l.

Mons. Deschap. My dear child,
How shall I thank—how bless thee? Thou hast saved—
I will not say my fortune—I could bear
Reverse, and shrink not—but that prouder wealth
Which merchants value most—my name, my credit—
The hard-won honors of a toilsome life—
These thou hast saved, my child !
   Pauline. Is there no hope?
No hope but this ?
   Mons. Deschap. None. If, without the sum
Which Beauseant offers for thy hand, this day
Sinks to the west—to-morrow brings our ruin !
And hundreds, mingled in that ruin, curse
The bankrupt merchant ! and the insolent herd
We feasted and made merry, cry in scorn,
"How pride has fallen !—Lo, the bankrupt merchant !"
120. My daughter, thou hast saved us !
   Pauline. And am lost !
   Mons. Deschap. Come, let me hope that Beauseant's
     love——
   Pauline. His love !
Talk not of love—Love has no thought of self !
Love buys not with the ruthless usurer's gold
The loathsome prostitution of a hand
Without a heart ! Love sacrifices all things,
To bless the thing it loves ! *He* knows not love.
Father, his love is hate—his hope revenge !
My tears, my anguish, my remorse for falsehood—
These are the joys he wrings from our despair !
   121. *Mons. Deschap.* If thou deem'st thus, reject him !
     Shame and ruin
Were better than thy misery ;—think no more on't.

My sand is wellnigh run—what boots it when
The glass is broken ? We'll annul the contract;
And if to-morrow in the prisoner's cell
These aged limbs are laid, why still, my child,
I'll think thou art spared ; and wait the Liberal Hour
That lays the beggar by the side of kings !

    Pauline. No—no—forgive me ! You, my honor'd
        father,—
You, who so loved, so cherish'd me, whose lips
Never knew one harsh word ! I'm not ungrateful :
I am but human !—hush ! *Now,* call the bridegroom—
122. You see I am prepared—no tears—all calm ;
But, father, *talk no more of love !*

    Mons. Deschap. My child,
'Tis but one struggle; he is young, rich, noble ;
Thy state will rank first 'mid the dames of Lyons;
And when this heart can shelter thee no more
Thy youth will not be guardianless.

    Pauline. I have set
My foot upon the ploughshare—I will pass
The fiery ordeal.—(*Aside.*) Merciful Heaven, support
      me !
And on the absent wanderer shed the light
Of happier stars—lost ever more to me !

Enter MADAME DESCHAPPELLES, BEAUSEANT, GLAVIS, *and*
NOTARY, L. C.

123. *Madame Deschap.* Why, Pauline, you are quite in
deshabille—you ought to be more alive to the importance
of this joyful occasion. We had once looked higher, it
is true ; but you see, after all, Monsieur Beauseant's father
was a Marquis, and that's a great comfort ! Pedigree and
jointure !—you have them both in Monsieur Beauseant.
A young lady decorously brought up should only have two

considerations in her choice of a husband :—first, is his
birth honorable?—secondly, will his death be advantageous? All other trifling details should be left to parental
anxiety.

124. *Beauseant (approaching,. and waving aside* MA-
DAME). Ah, Pauline! let me hope that you are reconciled
to an event which confers such rapture upon me.

Pauline. I am reconciled to my doom.

Beauseant. Doom is a harsh word, sweet lady.

Pauline (aside). This man must have some mercy—his
heart cannot be marble. (*Aloud.*) Oh, sir, be just—be
generous!—Seize a noble triumph—a great revenge!—
Save the father, and spare the child!

Beauseant (aside). Joy—joy alike to my hatred and my
passion! The haughty Pauline is at last my suppliant.
125. (*Aloud.*) You ask from me what I have not the sublime virtue to grant—a virtue reserved only for the gardener's son! I cannot forego my hopes in the moment of
their fulfilment!—I adhere to the contract—your father's
ruin, or your hand!

Pauline. Then all is over. Sir, I have decided.

[*The clock strikes One.*

Enter DAMAS *and* MELNOTTE, L. C.

Damas. Your servant, cousin Deschappelles.—Let me
introduce Colonel Morier.

Madame Deschap. (curtseying very low). What, the celebrated hero? This is indeed an honor.

[MELNOTTE *bows and remains in the background.*

Damas (to PAULINE). My little cousin, I congratulate
you! What, no smile—no blush? You are going to be
divorced from poor Melnotte, and marry this rich gentleman. You ought to be excessively happy!

Pauline. Happy!

126. *Damas.* Why, how pale you are, child!—Poor Pauline! Hist—confide in me! Do they force you to this?

Pauline. No.

Damas. You act with your own free consent?

Pauline. My own consent—yes.

Damas. Then you are the most—I will not say what you are.

Pauline. You think ill of me—be it so—yet if you knew all——

Damas. There is some mystery. Speak out, Pauline.

Pauline (suddenly). Oh, perhaps you can save me! you are our relation—our friend. My father is on the verge of bankruptcy—this day he requires a large sum to meet demands that cannot be denied; that sum Beauseant will advance—this hand the condition of the barter. Save me, if you have the means—save me! You will be repaid above!

127. *Damas (aside).* I recant—women are not so bad, after all! *(Aloud.)* Humph, child! I cannot help you— I am too poor!

Pauline. The last plank to which I clung is shivered!

Damas. Hold—you see my friend Morier: Melnotte is his most intimate friend—fought in the same fields— slept in the same tent. Have you any message to send to Melnotte?—any word to soften this blow?

Pauline. He knows Melnotte—he will see him—he will bear to him my last farewell—*(approaches* MELNOTTE)— He has a stern air—he turns away from me—he despises me!—Sir, one word, I beseech you.

Melnotte. Her voice again! How the old time comes o'er me!

128. *Damas (to* MADAME). Don't interrupt him: He is going to tell her what a rascal young Melnotte is; he knows him well, I promise you.

Madame Deschap. So considerate in you, cousin Damas!

[DAMAS *approaches* DESCHAPPELLES; *converses apart with him in dumb show.*—DESCHAPPELLES *shows him a paper, which he inspects, and takes.*

Pauline. Thrice have I sought to speak—my courage
    fails me.
Sir, is it true that you have known—nay, are you
The friend of—Melnotte?
Melnotte. Lady, yes!—Myself
And Misery know the man!
Pauline. And you will see him,
And you will bear to him—ay, word for word,
All that this heart, which breaks in parting from him,
Would send, ere still forever.

129. *Melnotte.* He hath told me
You have the right to choose from out the world
A worthier bridegroom;—he foregoes all claim
Even to murmur at his doom. Speak on!
Pauline. Tell him, for years I never nursed a thought
That was not his; that on his wandering way,
Daily and nightly, pour'd a mourner's prayers.
Tell him ev'n now that I would rather share
His lowliest lot,—walk by his side, an outcast,—
Work for him, beg with him,—live upon the light
Of one kind smile from him,—than wear the crown
The Bourbon lost!

130. *Melnotte (aside).* Am I already mad?
And does delirium utter such sweet words
Into a dreamer's ear? (*Aloud.*) You love him thus,
And yet desert him?
Pauline. Say, that if his eye
Could read this heart,—its struggles, its temptations,—
His love itself would pardon that desertion!

8*

Look on that poor old man—he is my father;
He stands upon the verge of an abyss;
He calls his child to save him!   Shall I shrink
From him who gave me birth? withhold my hand,
And see a parent perish?   Tell him this,
And say—that we shall meet again in heaven!

131. *Melnotte (aside).* The night is past; joy cometh
     with the morrow.
(Aloud.) Lady—I—I—what is this riddle? what
The nature of this sacrifice?

Pauline (pointing to DAMAS). Go, ask him!

Beauseant (from the table). The papers are prepared—
     we only need
Your hand and seal.

Melnotte. Stay, lady!—one word more!
Were but your duty with your faith united,
Would you still share the low-born peasant's lot?

Pauline. Would I? Ah, better death with him I love
Than all the pomp—which is but as the flowers
That crown the victim!—*(turning away.)* I am ready.

               [MELNOTTE *rushes to* DAMAS.

132. *Damas.* There—
This is the schedule—this the total.

Beauseant (to DESCHAPPELLES, *showing notes).* These
Are yours the instant she has sign'd; you are
Still the great House of Lyons!

    [*The Notary is about to hand the contract to* PAULINE,
        when MELNOTTE *seizes and tears it.*

Beauseant. Are you mad?

Mons. Deschap. How, Sir! What means this insult?

Melnotte. Peace, old man!
I have a prior claim.   Before the face
Of man and Heaven I urge it! I outbid

Yon sordid huckster for your priceless jewel.

[*Giving a pocket-book.*

There is the sum twice told ! Blush not to take it :
There's not a coin that is not bought and hallow'd
In the cause of nations with a soldier's blood !

    Beauseant. Torments and death !

133. *Pauline.* That voice ! Thou art——

    Melnotte. Thy husband !

[PAULINE *rushes into his arms.*

    Melnotte. Look up ! Look up, Pauline !—for I can bear
Thine eyes ! The stain is blotted from my name.
I have redeem'd mine honor. I can call
On France to sanction thy divine forgiveness !
Oh, joy ! Oh, rapture ! By the midnight watch-fires
Thus have I seen thee !—thus foretold this hour !
And, 'midst the roar of battle, thus have heard
The beating of thy heart against my own !

134. *Beauseant.* Fool'd, duped, and triumph'd over
    in the hour
Of mine own victory ! Curses on ye both !
May thorns be planted in the marriage bed !
And love grow sour'd and blacken into hate,
Such as the hate that gnaws me !   [*Crosses to* L.

    Damas. Curse away !
And let me tell thee, Beauseant, a wise proverb
The Arabs have,—" Curses are like young chickens,

[*Solemnly.*

And still come home to roost !"

    Beauseant. Their happiness
Maddens my soul ! I am powerless and revengeless.

[*To* MADAME.

I wish you joy ! Ha ! ha ! the gardener's son ! [*Exit* L. C.

135. *Damas* (*to* GLAVIS). Your friend intends to hang
    himself ! Methinks
You ought to be his traveling companion !

Glavis. Sir, you are exceedingly obliging! [*Exit* L. C.
Pauline. Oh!
My father, you are saved,—and by my husband!
Ah! blesséd hour!

 Melnotte. Yet you weep still, Pauline!

 Pauline. But on thy breast!—*these* tears are sweet and
  holy!

 Mons. Deschap. You have won love and honor, nobly,
  sir!
Take her;—be happy both!

 Madame Deschap. I'm all astonish'd!
Who, then, is Colonel Morier?

 Damas. You behold him!

 Melnotte. Morier no more after this happy day!
136. I would not bear again my father's name
Till I could deem it spotless! The hour's come!
Heaven smiled on Conscience! As the soldier rose
From rank to rank, how sacred was the fame
That cancell'd crime, and raised him nearer thee!

 Madame Deschap. A colonel and a hero! Well, that's
  something!
He's wondrously improved! I wish you joy, sir!

 Melnotte. Ah! the same love that tempts us into sin,
If it be true love, works out its redemption!
And he who seeks repentance for the Past
Should woo the Angel Virtue in the future!

PICTURE.

MELNOTTE.

  PAULINE.   MADAME D.
DAMAS.   MONSIEUR D.
 R. R. C. C. L. C. L.

The Curtain falls.

TROISIÈME PARTIE.

SUJETS DE COMPOSITIONS ORIGINALES,

POUVANT SERVIR ÉGALEMENT POUR

DICTÉES ET VERSIONS.

(93)

SUJETS DE

COMPOSITIONS ORIGINALES.

N.B. Les titres indiquent, non le sujet de la lettre, mais celui de la réponse à y faire.

1. Description d'une personne au physique et au moral.

(Sujet donné à l'Université d'Oxford, 1866. Senior Candidates.)

MONSIEUR,—J'ai parmi mes connaissances plusieurs jeunes gens du nom de Lebrun ; donc, si vous désirez que je vous donne des renseignements sur la famille de la personne qui s'est présentée chez vous, il faut absolument que vous m'en fassiez la description au physique et au moral. Vous pouvez écrire avec confiance, et compter sur ma discrétion. J'ai l'honneur de vous saluer.

---

2. Parties d'Enfants à la Campagne.

A Mesdames C. M. R., organisatrices des excursions à la campagne, en faveur des enfants pauvres.

Washington, 10 Juillet, 1872.

MESDAMES,—Nous apprenons que votre heureuse idée d'offrir aux enfants pauvres de votre ville des parties de

(95)

plaisir ou excursions à la campagne, est sur le point de se réaliser.

Nous vous serions très-obligées de nous envoyer une relation détaillée de votre première excursion et des effets salutaires qu'elle aura produits sur vos jeunes protégés.

Cette communication, intéressante à tous les points de vue, nous aidera à former ici un Comité à l'instar du vôtre.

Veuillez agréer, Mesdames, etc. etc.

---

3. Une Soirée dans une Pension de jeunes filles.

Mademoiselle Louise Newman, Élève à la Pension de Madame C.

New-York, 20 Sept. 1872.

MA CHÈRE LOUISE,—J'ai reçu l'invitation que l'aimable Directrice de votre pension m'a fait l'honneur de m'envoyer, pour votre soirée d'ouverture de jeudi prochain. Le programme est, certes, des plus attrayants : Une comédie de Scribe, jouée par les élèves ; puis, des danses qui n'en finiront pas.

A mon grand regret, je ne pourrai y assister, car notre chère mère, bien que complètement rétablie, réclame encore ma présence.

Mais j'attends de toi, *en français*, aussitôt que tu seras remise de tes fatigues, une description complète de cette soirée mémorable, avec tous les détails que te fournira ta brillante imagination de pensionnaire.

En te lisant, il me semblera que j'y assiste, et je me croirai encore au milieu de mes chères amies de l'année dernière.

Je te prie de présenter à Madame C. mes excuses, mes regrets et mes remercîments.

Ta sœur qui t'aime,

AMÉLIE.

4. Incendie dans un Port de Mer.

École Navale des États-Unis, Mai 1872.

.   .   .   .

P.S.—Au moment où je termine ma lettre dans le salon-fumoir de la première classe, Barber vient lire à la chambrée le télégramme assez circonstancié qui annonce le magnifique sauvetage du port et de la ville de Marseille par l'escadre des Etats-Unis. Il paraît que les "Middies" commandaient, avec autant de sang-froid qu'à la parade, les embarcations qui ont abordé et coulé le navire espagnol bondé de pétrole. Envoyez-nous des détails complets sur cette action d'éclat qui fait tant d'honneur à la marine américaine.

Nous avons déjà poussé les trois hourrahs traditionnels, et avec tant d'entrain que vous avez dû les entendre par-delà l'Atlantique. Nous les renouvellerons à la réception de votre missive que nous attendons impatiemment par le retour du steamer.

Rogers H. Galt.

---

5. Distribution de Brevets à l'École militaire.

Nos examens de fin d'année m'ont tellement fatigué, mon cher Colonel, que je ne pourrais vous donner les détails que vous me demandez sur la distribution des Brevets aux Cadets qui viennent de terminer leur cours. Mais votre ami Julius, à qui j'ai communiqué votre lettre (et qui a eu constamment la première place en français), se charge de vous les donner, et *dans sa langue maternelle*, a-t-il ajouté, non sans fierté. Sa lettre suivra de près la

mienne. Nous vous attendons avec impatience, vous et
votre famille, sur les bords enchantés de l'Hudson.

A vous.

6-9. Les Plaisirs de chaque Saison.

6.—Le Printemps.
7.—L'Été.
8.—L'Automne.
9.—L'Hiver.

MES CHERS ENFANTS,—Votre père se plaint amèrement,
—et, entre nous, il n'a pas tout-à-fait tort,—que vos
demandes d'argent pour vos menus-plaisirs vont toujours
en augmentant. Il m'a positivement défendu de lui com-
muniquer aucune de vos lettres contenant des demandes
de cette nature. Il prétend que votre tante vous gâte ;
qu'elle vous traite comme si vous étiez de grandes per-
sonnes, tandis que, selon lui, vous n'êtes encore et ne
devez être que des enfants ; que vous dépensez à vous
deux comme quatre, etc. Il menace de vous retirer de
chez votre tante et de vous placer, comme internes, dans
vos pensions respectives.

Ce serait, pour ma bonne sœur et pour vous, un véritable coup de foudre.

J'ai fait de mon mieux l'office de paratonnerre ; et, en
le prenant par son faible, j'ai tourné la difficulté.

Voici son ultimatum :

Vous savez quel prix il attache à l'étude du français.
Désormais vous ne ferez aucune demande directe d'argent ;
mais à chaque saison vous décrirez, dans *une lettre en français*, chacun de votre côté, les divers plaisirs qui vous at-
tendent et dont vous espérez jouir.

Ces lettres lui seront soumises, et si elles le satisfont, il vous enverra, comme par le passé, le nerf de la guerre. Voilà ce que j'ai pu obtenir; à vous de faire le reste.

N'oubliez pas que votre père possède à fond cette langue qu'il aime tant. Sa générosité se mesurera à la correction grammaticale et à l'élégance du style. Lisez beaucoup ; étudiez sans relâche votre syntaxe ; car, tout anglicisme, tout solécisme aurait une fâcheuse influence sur ses décisions, et par ricochet, sur vos plaisirs.

Je suis assez rassurée en ce qui concerne Marie ; mais toi, Maurice, tu me sembles avoir beaucoup à faire.

Toutefois, mes chers enfants, ayez bon courage. "Travaillez, prenez de la peine,"—et . . . les fonds ne vous manqueront pas. N'est-ce pas Lafontaine qui dit cela?

Je vous embrasse tous deux avec tendresse, mes bien-aimés, et je vous prie d'embrasser pour moi votre excellente tante. Votre père, apaisé par la perspective des *lettres françaises*, se joint à moi et m'autorise à vous le dire.

A vous, mes chers enfants, tout notre amour.

ADRIENNE G.

P.S.—Bien entendu, vos lettres devront être l'œuvre de chacun de vous, sans aide de qui que ce soit ; sans retouches et sans corrections autres que celles que vous ferez vous-mêmes.

---

10. Lettre de Recommandation.

À MM. L. et Cie, Éditeurs.

Paris, ce 25 Janvier, 1873.

MESSIEURS,—La santé de mon père est toujours chancelante et précaire. Depuis que ma sœur est mariée au loin, je reste à peu près seul pour lui donner les soins que son état réclame. Mon retour en Amérique se trouve ainsi indéfiniment ajourné.　Je me vois donc, à mon grand regret, obligé de vous envoyer ma démission de la place que j'occupe depuis dix années dans votre honorable Maison.

J'apprends à l'instant qui'une place de confiance est en ce moment vacante chez MM. Hachette et Cie, libraires de l'Université.　Ma connaissance de l'anglais et d1 français me donnerait quelque chance de l'obtenir.

Me rappelant vos bontés passées, je viens, Messieurs, vous prier d'y mettre le sceau, en écrivant à MM. Hachette et en leur donnant sur moi, sur mes connaissances spéciales en librairie, et sur la confiance que l'on peut avoir en moi, tous les détails que vous suggéreront votre amitié et votre bienveillance pour moi.

Daignez accepter, Messieurs, avec mes regrets bien sentis d'être obligé de me séparer de vous, et mes remerciments et l'expression de mon profond respect.

EMILE BONNARD.

11.　Lettre de Remercîment.

Émile Bonnard, à Nice, France.

Mars 2, 1873.

Reçu par télégraphe réponse Hachette.　Vous êtes accepté.　Ils veulent que soyons premiers à vous annoncer cette bonne nouvelle.　Félicitations.

L. ET CIE.

---

12. Une Traversée sur l'Atlantique.

M. BÉNIGNE VUILLEMOT, à bord du *Lafayette*, aux soins de M. le Capitaine S.

Impossible, cher ami, d'être à bord ce matin pour te

serrer une dernière fois la main. Mais j'espère que tu penseras à moi pendant la traversée.

Prends note de tous les incidents à bord ; et aussitôt arrivé au Hâvre jette à la poste un récit bien circonstancié de votre traversée.

Ta lettre portant le timbre du Hâvre m'indiquera que tu es arrivé à bon port.

C'est ce que souhaite de tout son cœur

Ton ami,

VICTOR JULLIEN.

---

13. Incendie d'une Ville.

À MM. F. Fisher et Cie., négociants, Chicago.

Télégrammes effrayants arrivent d'heure en heure.—Vîte, détails généraux.—Craignez-vous pour votre maison ?—Détails sur vos familles, vos enfants.—Envoyons secours par train-éclair, Erié.—Ardentes sympathies de New-York.—Ecrivez aussitôt que possible.

J. LEWIS.

---

14. Un Bal à Versailles—Toilettes.

Eh quoi, ma chère Nellie, c'est par les journaux que votre ancienne institutrice apprend la brillante réception qui vous a été faite à la Cour . . républicaine de France. Voyons, tâchez de vous soustraire, ne fut-ce qu'une heure, aux énivrements des fêtes, et donnez-moi force détails sur le bal, sur les toilettes, sur *tout*, et sur *tous*.

Mais n'oubliez point que je ne comprends absolument qu'une langue, le Francais, et n'allez pas émailler votre lettre d'expressions anglo-saxonnes.

A vous de cœur,

VICTOIRE MONNIER.

9*

15. La Nöel au Collége.

Master Philippe Richard, 1ère Prép. au Collége de Ste. Marie-aux-Monts.

Baltimore, 20 Décembre, 1871.

Mon bien-aimé Philippe,—Je suis très-heureuse d'apprendre que tu te remets petit-à-petit de ta longue indisposition et que tu espères être entièrement guéri, juste pour les fêtes de Noël. Mon vieil et révérend ami a mis au bas de ton Bulletin mensuel que tu te portes comme le Pont-Neuf. Mais tu sais, mon précieux Philippe, je n'ai nulle confiance dans les Présidents de Collége. Ils ne comprennent rien aux enfants.

Afin de hâter ta convalescence, je t'envoie par les Messageries Adams une caisse de bonbons et de friandises.

Mais, uses-en avec modération, à cause de ta faible santé. Je te dis cela parceque j'ai cru remarquer en toi un petit faible pour la gourmandise.

Ecris-moi si la caisse est arrivée en bon état, et dis-moi comment tu as trouvé son contenu. Aussi comment tu as passé les fêtes de Noël.

Soigne-toi toujours bien, et ne travaille pas de façon à te rendre malade.

Ta vieille grand'-mère, qui n'aime que son Philippe au monde,

Priscille Richard.

---

16. Lettre de Condoléance.

Monsieur et cher ami,—Accablé de douleur, je ne puis que vous écrire ces deux lignes pour vous annoncer la perte que nous venons de faire en la personne de notre bien-aimé père. Il est mort cette nuit, après cette longue et douloureuse maladie, qu'il a tout le temps supportée avec le courage et la resignation d'un chrétien. Il souffrait tellement dans les derniers temps que c'est presque une grâce que Dieu lui a faite en le rappelant à Lui. Mais le coup n'en est pas moins sensible pour nous tous.

Pourrez-vous assister à la triste cérémonie, qui aura lieu après-demain à 10 heures?

Si non, écrivez-moi. Une lettre du meilleur ami de mon père et qui me parlera de lui, ne pourra que me faire du bien. Adieu, à bientôt,

LUCIEN B.

M. LEBRUN, Elizabeth City, N. J.

---

17. Suicide.
18. Emeute.
19. Accident de chemin de fer.
20. Mass-meeting.
21. Régates.
22. Première représentation de Faust.
23. Sermon.

À MM. les Reporters de *l'Echo Français.*

Ordre de la Semaine:

ON annonce le *suicide* d'une jeune fille rue Sacramento; aussi une *émeute* sanglante au quartier chinois.

On parle également d'un sérieux *accident* sur le chemin de fer du Pacifique.

Voyez ce qu'il y a de fondé dans ces rumeurs.

Mardi aura lieu un *mass-meeting* sur la principale place. Jeudi, *régates.*

Le lendemain, *première représentation* de FAUST, à l'Académie de Musique.

Dimanche, prendre des notes sur le *Sermon* que le Révérend P. Deneuf doit prêcher à l'Eglise St. Augustin. Veuillez, Messieurs, envoyer la copie en temps utile.

Agréez, etc.,

LE DIRECTEUR.

---

24. Partie de Chasse.

À M. le Marquis Hubert de Villers, au château de C.

J'APPRENDS, heureux Nemrod, que vous passez tout votre temps à chasser. Et vous ne m'envoyez ni un bout de lettre, ni une pièce de conviction,—je veux dire un lièvre ou un chevreuil assassinés par vous.

Votre cœur, endurci par le carnage quotidien, se rendra-t-il à l'appel de l'amitié?

Allons, ôtez vos guêtres de peau de daim et vos gants *idem* et écrivez-moi longuement.

Sur ce, je prie votre Patron de vous avoir en sa sainte et digne garde.

GASTON.

---

25. Partie de Pêche.

À M. le Comte G. de Laferrière, au Val-Suzon.

ASSASSIN vous-même, mon cher Gaston! vous pêcheur et pêcheur endurci!

Vos passe-temps là-bas sont-ils donc si innocents?

Que vous ont fait ces belles carpes pour les faire pâmer sur l'herbe en attendant la poële à frire? Que vous ont fait ces délicieuses truites saumonées pour les accommoder à la chambord? Et ces superbes écrevisses à pattes rouges que vous plongerez toutes vivantes dans la chaudière, comme au 5ème acte de *La Juive?*

Faisons un marché :

Après-demain vous m'enverrez une longue description de vos parties de pêche, avec truites et écrevisses à l'appui ; et moi, je remettrai au messager, en échange, une bourriche de venaison, avec lettre explicative.

Cela vous va-t-il ?   A vous,
                                                                        HUBERT.

---

26. Ressources que l'Amérique offre aux émigrants.
27. Rapide extension de ses voies ferrées.
28. Principaux traits de mœurs des Américains.

À M. E. LONGUEMARE, St. Louis, Missouri, États-Unis.

Strasbourg, 20 Juillet, 1872.

MONSIEUR ET AMI,—La guerre qui vient de se terminer et dont l'issue a été si fatale à notre malheureuse France, a sensiblement diminué ma fortune.   Ayant opté pour la nationalité française, je ne suis plus magistrat.

Mais, vous le savez, j'ai toujours eu beaucoup de goût pour l'agriculture, et je pense que mes connaissances spéciales en cette matière peuvent être utilisées par moi au profit de ma nombreuse famille.

Notre intention est d'émigrer aux Etats-Unis, aussitôt que j'aurai pu réaliser les épaves sauvées du naufrage.

Je vous serais donc obligé de vouloir bien m'adresser, aussitôt que vos occupations vous le permettront, une description assez complète des avantages que l'Amérique peut offrir aux étrangers, spécialement le " Far-West."

La terre est-elle aussi fertile et à aussi bon marché qu'on le dit ?

Avez-vous, dans l'ouest, de bonnes voies de communication et des débouchés faciles pour vos denrées ?   Les

E*

objets de première nécessité y sont-ils chers? Donnez-moi un aperçu des prix.

Décrivez-nous aussi les populations au milieu desquelles nous nous proposons d'aller planter notre tente; leurs mœurs, leurs habitudes, leurs défauts et leurs qualités.

Voilà une rude tâche que nous imposons à l'amitié; mais nous savons que nous pouvons compter sur la vôtre. D'ailleurs vous pouvez nous donner tous ces détails en plusieurs lettres.

Nous sommes tous en bonne santé; mes fils sont pleins de courage et mes filles prétendent qu'elles feront d'excellentes fermières. Ma femme seule, qui n'a jamais perdu de vue la flèche de la Cathédrale, hésite encore à entreprendre un si long voyage. Mais les renseignements que vous nous donnerez, triompheront sans nul doute de ses hésitations, et j'espère, Dieu aidant, que nous irons bientôt tous nous échouer sur vos côtes hospitalières.

Bien à vous,

De Reffemberg.

---

29. Appel aux Professeurs de français aux Etats-Unis.

Mesdames, Messieurs,—L'auteur des sujets de compositions qui précèdent, ne pouvait songer à assumer, seul et sans aide, la tâche qu'il a entreprise.

Si vous pensez que ces courtes lettres en français, qui provoquent à une réponse dans la même langue, peuvent former la base d'un exercice attrayant et profitable pour vos élèves, nous vous prions de leur demander de composer elles-mêmes (ou eux-mêmes) de nouvelles lettres dans le même genre, et de nous adresser, après correction, celles que vous jugerez les mieux réusssies.

Nous en enrichirons notre prochaine édition.

De cette façon et en faisant appel à tous les concours, nous pourrons obtenir une grande variété de *sujets* et de *styles*,—*variété* si désirable en pareille matière.

Comptez à l'avance sur notre reconnaissance.

Vos très-respectueux et très-dévoués serviteurs,

LES EDITEURS.

VOCABULARY.

ABBREVIATIONS.

adj., adjective.
adv., adverb.
aft., after.
art., article.
bef., before.
conj., conjunction.
dem., demonstrative.
excl., exclamation.
f., feminine.
fam., familiar.
id., idiomatic.
ind., indicative.
inf., infinitive.
int., interjection.

m., masculine.
m., f., of both genders.
num., numeral.
p. *or* pl., plural.
part., participle.
poss., possessive.
prep., preposition.
pres., present.
pron., pronoun.
prov., proverb.
s., substantive, *and, occasionally*, singular.
v., verb.
vulg., vulgar.

A 1 at the top of a verb of the first conjugation, like *mener* 1, refers the student to § 5, 6, 7, or 8 of the Rules, sect. 1, headed *Remarks concerning the Verbs of the First Conjugation.*

A dagger (†) before a verb, like † *mettre*, indicates that such verb is irregular, and that it will be found in the list of irregular verbs, pages 23 to 27. When in the middle of a verb, like *pro†mettre*, it refers the student to the simple form of the verb, *mettre.*

An apostrophe (') before a word commencing with an *h* shows that this *h* is mute, and reminds the student of the rules of elision.

A number between parentheses (25) indicates from what section of the text the sentence quoted is extracted.

GRAMMATICAL AND IDIOMATICAL

VOCABULARY

TO BULWER'S LADY OF LYONS.

A, AN, art. ind. *un, une.*
The article A is not translated in French : 1. When the noun (generally predicate to the verb *être*) is used adjectively : I am still *a* bachelor, *je suis encore garçon* ; 2. After *what* or *such*, in exclamations : what *a* coward! *quel poltron!* and such a love! *et quel amour!*

ABHOR, v. *abhorrer.*

ABOUT, adv. *environ ; çà et là ;* bustling —, (63) *allant et venant çà et là.*

ABOUT, prep. 1. *sur, de ;* about Melnotte, *sur* or *de M. ;* 2. (fig.) — her, *en elle ;* 3. (on the eve of), *sur le point de ; —* to depart, *sur le point de partir ;* what are you about? (30) *qu'allez-vous faire?*

ABOVE, adv. *en haut ;* from —, *d'en haut ;* (in heaven), *là haut, au ciel.*

ABOVE, prep. *au-dessus de.*

ABSTRACTION, s. (of mind), *distraction, préoccupation,* f.

ABYSS, s. *abîme,* m.

ACCEPT, v. *accepter.*

ACCORDING, prep. *suivant ; —* as, *suivant que ; —* to, *suivant, selon.*

ACCOUNT, s. *compte,* m. ; account-book, *grand-livre, journal.*

ACQUIRE, v. †*acquérir.*

ACT, s. *acte,* m.

ACT, v. *agir ; —* ill, *mal agir.*

ACTUALLY, adv. *réellement, effectivement.*

ADD, v. *ajouter.*

ADDITIONAL, adj. *additionnel, de plus ;* an — clerk, *un commis de plus.*

ADDRESS, s. *adresse,* f.

ADHERE, v. *s'en* †*tenir, adhérer* (to, *à*).

ADMIT, v. *ad†mettre, ac†cueillir qqn. chez soi, laisser entrer.*

ADORER, s. *adorateur, -trice ;* I grew, what to the last I shall be, thine —, *je grandis—ce que je serai jusqu'à la fin—ton adorateur ;* or, better, *je te vouai dès lors un véritable culte, qui durera toujours.*

ADRIATIC, s. *Adriatique,* f.

ADVANCE, v. *avancer¹, s'avancer¹.*

ADVANTAGE, s. *avantage,* m. ; to the best —, *au mieux de nos intérêts.*

ADVANTAGEOUS, adj. *avantageux.*

AFFAIR, s. *affaire,* f.

AFFRONT, v. 1. (to face), *affronter ;* 2. (outrage, insult), *outrager qqn.,* †*faire un affront à qqn.*

AFRAID, adj. *effrayé ;* to be —, *avoir peur* (of, *de*); (that, *que,* subj.).

AFTER, adv. *après ; —* all, *après tout ;* let us —, (33) *allons après.*

AFTER, conj. *après que ; —* I have fought, (46) *après que je me suis battu.*

AGAIN, adv. 1. *encore, de nouveau, à nouveau ;* 2. (with a neg.), *plus, plus jamais ;* I will not speak to you —, *je ne vous parlerai plus jamais.*
Again is often rendered by the prefix *re :* we live — in our children, *nous* REvivons *dans nos enfants.*

AGAINST, prep. *contre ; —* it, *là contre* (abs.).

AGED, adj. *vieux, âgé ;* (*vieux* bef. and *âgé* after the noun).

AGITATED, part. *agité.*

AGO, *il y a ;* three years —, *il y a trois ans* (note the transposition); not an hour —, *il y a à peine une heure.*

AGONY, s. (of death), *agonie,* f. ; (of sufferings), *excès de.*

AIR, s. *air,* m.; *atmosphère,* f.; every — is heavy with sighs, (39) *l'atmosphère est chargée,* or, *imprégnée de soupirs ;* (fig.), to give oneself airs, *se donner des airs.*

AISLE, s. (of a church), *aîle,* f., *bas-côté,* m.

ALABASTER, s. *albâtre,* m.

ALARMED, part. ; to be —, *s'alarmer, être alarmé.*

ALIKE, adj. *égal, pareil* (to, *à*).

ALIKE, adv. 1. *de même ;* 2. (together), *de compagnie, ensemble.*

ALIVE, adj. *vivant ;* to be — to the importance of, (123) *être pénétré de l'importance de.*

ALL, adj. *tout ;* pl., m., *tous.* How is — this to end? *comment tout cela finira-t-il? —* of you, *vous tous ;* after —, *après tout.*

ALLAY, v. *calmer.*

ALLOW, v. *per†mettre qch. à qqn.* (*de,* inf.).

ALLOY, s. *alliage,* m.

ALMOST, adv. 1. (nearly), *presque ;* 2. (entirely), *tout-à-fait.*

ALONE, adj. *seul.*

ALONE, adv. (only), *seulement ;* there —, *là seulement.*

ALOUD, adv. *haut.*

ALPINE, adj. *des Alpes* (lit., *of the Alps*).

ALREADY, adv. *déjà.*

ALSO, adv. *aussi, de même.*

ALTAR, s. *autel,* m.

ALTER, v. *changer[1] ;* — the position of a rose, *changer une rose de place.*

ALWAYS, adv. *toujours.*

AMBITIOUS, adj. *ambitieux.*

AMIDST, prep. *parmi, dans, au milieu de.*

AMONG, prep. *parmi.*

AMUSE, v. *amuser, s'amuser* (to, *à*).

ANCESTORS, s. pl. *ancêtres,* m. pl.

ANCESTRY, s. *lignage,* m., *ancêtres,* m. pl.

AND, conj. *et. And* is not translated after *go : go and* order the carriage, *allez donner l'ordre d'atteler.*

ANGEL, s. *ange,* m.; (voc.) *ô doux ange !*

ANGUISH, s. *angoisse,* f. (more used in the pl., *angoisses*).

ANNUL, v. *annuler.*

ANON, adv. *tout-à-l'heure.*

ANOTHER, adj. *autre ;* she is —'s, *elle est à un autre.*

ANSWER, s. *réponse,* f.

ANSWER, v. *répondre* (for, *de*).

ANXIETY, s. *anxiété, soins anxieux,* m. pl.; to parental —, *aux soins anxieux des parents.*

ANY, adj. *du, de la, de l', des ; aucun ; n'importe quel ;* have you not — relations in Lyons? *n'avez-vous pas de parents à L. ?* or, *n'avez-vous aucun parent à L. ? —* reason will convince him, *n'importe quelle raison le convaincra ;* any one (affirm.), *qui que ce soit, n'importe qui ;* (negat.), *personne ; —* one might see, *n'importe qui peut voir ;* I do not know — one in the family, *je ne connais personne de la famille ; —* thing (affirm.), *quoi que ce soit ;* (negat.), *rien ;* except — thing that is useful, (5) *excepté quoi que ce soit d'utile ;* he did not suspect — thing, *il ne soupçonna rien.*

APART, adv. *à part.*

APOLLO, s. *Apollon,* m.

APPALLING, adj. *terrible, douloureux.*

APPEAL, v. *en appeler[1].* I — to you, *j'en appelle à vous.*

APPEAR, v. †*paraître, sembler.*

APPEND, v. (a seal), *apposer* (*un sceau*).

APPETITE, s. *appétit,* m.

APPLY, v. *appliquer.*

APPOINTMENT, s. *nomination,* f.; to have the — of the establishment of, (9) *être chargé de former la maison de.*

APPROACH, v. *s'approcher* (*de*).

ARAB, s. *Arabe,* m.

ARCHING, adj. *en forme d'arcades.*

ARM, s. (limb), *bras,* m.

ARM, v. (oneself), *s'armer, s'armer de courage.*

ARMY, s. *armée,* f.; the Grand —, *la Grande Armée.*

ARREST, s. *arrestation.* f.; they will order his —, (48) *ils donneront l'ordre de l'arrêter.*

ARREST, v. *arrêter.*

ARRIVE, v. *arriver.*

AS, conj. (like), *comme;* as you say, *comme vous dites;* as it is, *dans l'état de choses actuel, dans la circonstance;* (viewing that), *comme, attendu que, vû que;* (bef. an adj.), *aussi;* as good, *aussi bon;* as silent as, *aussi silencieux que;* as cloudless as, *sans nuages comme;* — if, *comme si;* (in the shape of), *en qualité de, en, à titre de;* as a general, *en général,* or, *en tenue de général;* to see somebody as an acquaintance, *voir,* or, *recevoir qqn. à titre de connaissance;* as the prince of Como, (25) *sous le nom,* or, *en qualité de Prince de Côme;* (progression), as the soldier rose, *à mesure que le soldat montait en grade;* as for, *quant à;* so as, such as, (see So and Such.)

ASCEND, v. *monter, remonter.*

ASH, s. *cendre,* f.

ASHAMED, adj. *honteux;* to be —, *avoir honte, être honteux, rougir* (of, *de*).

ASIDE, adv. *à part.*

ASK, v. *demander (quelque chose à quelqu'un,* lit., something to somebody); (from, *à;*) I may — you a favor, (46) *je puis avoir à vous demander une faveur.*

ASSENT, s. *assentiment,* m.

ASSOCIATIONS, s. pl. *souvenirs,* m. pl.

ASTONISHED, part. *étonné;* I am —, *je tombe de mon haut,* id.

ASTRAY, adv. *hors de la voie;* to lead —, †*mettre hors de la bonne voie;* to go —, *se fourvoyer*[1].

AT, prep. *à;* at Lyons, *à Lyon;* — school, *à l'école.*

ATONE, v. *expier;* the energy to —, (79) *l'énergie de l'expiation.*

ATONEMENT, s. *expiation,* f.; let me come to such most poor —, (71) *venons à cette expiation, bien pauvre à la vérité.*

ATTACHMENT, s. *attachement,* m., *affection,* f.

ATTEMPT, s. *tentative,* f., *essai,* m. (at, *de*).

AUDIBLE, adj. *qu'on peut entendre.*

AUNT, s. *tante,* f.; my maiden —'s legacy, (30) *le legs de ma tante, la vieille fille.*

AUSTRIAN, adj. *autrichien.*

AUTHOR, s. *auteur,* m.

AUTHORIZE, v. *autoriser.*

AVENGE, v. *venger*[1].

AWARE, adj. *instruit de, qui sait, qui connaît.*

AWAY, adv. and int.; — with you! *hors d'ici! arrière!*

AWHILE, adv. *un instant, quelque temps.*

AWKWARD, adj. *maladroit.* He is an — fellow to deal with, (57) *c'est un dangereux compagnon, n'ayons rien à démêler avec lui,* or, *n'ayons pas noise avec lui.*

AY, int. *oui, que dis-je.*

B.

BABY, s. *bébé,* m.

BACHELOR, s. (unmarried), *garçon, célibataire,* m.

BACK, s. *derrière,* m.; (theatr.), *fond,* m.; background, *arrière-plan,* m.; in the —, *à l'arrière, à l'écart;* to be —, *être de retour. Back* is sometimes expressed by the French prefix *re:* to come —, RE†*venir.*

BAD, adj. *mauvais.*

BADGE, s. (of love), *gage d'amour,* m.

BAFFLE, v. †*faire échouer.*

BAIT, v. †*faire rafraîchir.*

BAKER, s. *boulanger, -ère.*

BALL, s. (dancing), *bal,* m.

BANKRUPT, adj. *failli, banqueroutier,* m.; — merchant, *marchand en faillite.*

BANKRUPTCY, s. *faillite, banqueroute,* f.

BARRACK, s. *caserne,* f.

BARTER, s. *marché,* m.

BASE, adj. *bas, dégradé;* — born, *de basse extraction.*

BATHE, v. *baigner, se baigner.*

BATTLE, s. *bataille,* f.

BE, v. aux. *être.*

The auxiliary verb *to be* forms in English many idioms which are to be rendered in French by corresponding idiomatic expressions, in the following manner:

1. (necessity, obligation, futurity), *devoir,* †*aller, être sur le point de,* or, *à la veille de; se disposer à;* she is to sign, *elle doit signer;* what is to become of Pauline? (47) *que va devenir P.?* not a moment is to be wasted, (48) *il n'y a pas un moment à perdre;* she was to have known all, (65) *elle aurait dû tout savoir;* he was to go to Paris, *il se disposait à aller à P.;* give your arm to her Highness that is to be, (51) *offrez votre bras à celle qui est sur le point* (or, *qui est à la veille*) *d'être son altesse;* — for; it is not for a mother to, *ce n'est pas à une mère à;* I am in no humor for, *je ne suis pas d'humeur à* (inf.).

2. (age), — thirty, (46) *avoir trente ans.*

3. (*were,* subj. conditional and hypothetical clauses), were your duty, *si votre devoir était;* it were, *ce serait;* (exclam.), that I were dead, *que ne suis-je mort!* (See IF.)

4. (unipersonal), it is too real, *ce n'est que trop réel;* it is you, *c'est vous;* that is not love, (40) *ce n'est pas là de l'amour;* they are my last words, (101) *ce sont mes dernières paroles;* it is so pleasant, (36) *il est si agréable;* it is our fathers that, (36) *ce sont nos pères que;* it would be so ill bred, (34) *ce serait si mal élevé,* or, *better, ce serait de si mauvais ton;* as it is, (24) *au point où en sont les choses;* though it is not many days since, (23) *bien qu'il ne soit arrivé que depuis quelques jours;* it is as true as, *c'est aussi vrai que;* it is a true sign, *c'est un signe certain;* it will be all over Lyons, *ce sera connu de tout L.,* or, *ce sera la fable de L.;* it must be, *ce* (or, *cela*) *doit être;* it is too late, *il est trop tard;* it is astonishing how much, (46) *c'est étonnant comme,* or *combien.*

BEAR, v. 1. (to lead), †*conduire,*

mener[1], *amener*[1] (to, *à*); —her home, *conduis-la chez toi;* 2. — the name, *porter le nom;* 3. (a grief), *supporter,* †*souffrir;* I can — thine eyes, *je puis supporter ton regard;* 4. with (together), *souffrir avec qqn.;* — with (to have patience), *avoir de l'indulgence pour, être indulgent pour, user de patience envers;* 5. the lady who bore me, (44) *la dame qui m'a donné le jour.*

BEARER, s. *porteur,* m.

BEAT, v. †*battre;* beating of a heart, *battement du cœur,* m.

BEAUTIFIER, s. *embellisseur,* m.

BEAUTIFUL, adj. *beau,* f. irreg. *belle* (*bel* is another form for *beau* used before a word commencing with a vowel or an *h* mute), *magnifique.*

BEAUTY, s. *beauté,* f.; a village —, *une beauté de village, une beauté campagnarde;* the — of Lyons, *la belle Lyonnaise;* all the beauties in L., *tout ce qu'il y a de beautés à L.*

BECAUSE, conj. *parce que.*

BECOME, v. *de*†*venir, se* †*faire;* to — eternal, *devenir éternel;* what has — of him? *qu'est-il devenu?*

BED, s. *lit,* m.; marriage —, *lit nuptial.*

BEE, s. *abeille,* f.

BEFORE, adv. (used absolut.), *auparavant.*

BEFORE, conj. *avant que* (subj.); before the ceremony is over, (50) *avant que la cérémonie soit finie.*

BEFORE, prep. *avant, devant;* (bef. an inf.), *avant de.*

BEG, v. 1. *demander* (*qch. à qqn.*), *prier;* he begs you will have, *il vous prie d'avoir;* 2. (mendicate), *mendier.*

BEGGAR, s. adj. *mendiant.*

BEGIN, v. *commencer*[1] (à bef. inf.).

BEGONE, int. *retirez-vous; arrière.*

BEHAVE, v. *se* †*conduire;* — ill, *se conduire mal.*

BEHOLD, v., prep. in Fr., *voici, voilà;* you — him, *vous l'avez devant les yeux.*

BELIEF, s. *croyance,* f.

BELIEVE, v. †*croire;* can I — my eyes? (21) *en puis-je croire mes yeux?*

BELOVED, part. and adj. *bien aimé.*

BENEATH, adv. *dessous.*

BENEATH, prep. *sous;* — thy smile, *sous ton sourire; au-dessous de.*

BESEECH, v. *supplier;* I — you, *je vous en supplie.*

BESIDE, prep. *à côté de;* — the sofa, *à côté du sofa.*

BESIDES, adv. *en outre.*

BEST, sup. *le meilleur* (sup. irreg. of *bon*).

BETRAY, v. *trahir.*

BETRAYER, s. *traître,* m.; I was her —, (56) *je l'ai trahie.*

BETTER, comp. *meilleur* (comp. irreg. of *bon*).

BETTER, adv. *mieux, plutôt;* — death than, *plutôt la mort que;* to be —, †*valoir mieux;* — to send for him hither, (10) *il vaut mieux le faire venir ici.*

BEWARE, int. *gare à vous!*

BEYOND, prep. *au delà de;* — the hour, (53) *au delà de l'heure présente.*

BIBLE, s. *Bible, f.*

BID, v. *demander (qch. à qqn.), ordonner, commander (de* bef. inf.); — me hope not! — me not hope! *demandez-moi de n'espérer plus, ne me demandez pas d'espérer.*

BILBO (lat.); for —, *de bilbo.*

BILL, s. (of fare), *carte,* f.

BIND, v. *lier;* (books), *relier.*

BIRTH, s. *naissance, origine,* f.; *rang,* m.

BITTER, adj. *amer, plein d'amertume;* this is indeed —, *voilà qui est amer en vérité.*

BITTERLY, adv. *amèrement.*

BLACKEN, v. *noircir.*

BLAME, s. *blâme,* m.

BLAME, v. *blâmer.*

BLAST, v. a†*battre,* †*faire du mal à;* 2. *flétrir, dessécher.*

BLAZON, s. *blason,* m.

BLEED, v. *saigner.*

BLESS, v. *bénir;* blessed hour, *heure bénie.*

BLESSING, s. *bénédiction, récompense,* f.

BLEST, part. *béni.*

BLIND, adj. *aveugle;* I was — to

all but her scorn, (42) *j'étais aveugle à tout* (or, *je ne voyais rien), si ce n'est son mépris.*

BLISS, s. *félicité,* f.

BLOCKHEAD, adj. and int. *tête dure!*

BLOOD, s. *sang,* m.

BLOSSOM, s. *floraison,* f., *épanouissement,* m.

BLOT, v. *effacer*[1] (from, *de*); — out, *effacer.*

BLOTTED, adj. *taché, barbouillé.*

BLOW, s. *coup,* m.

BLUBBER, v. *pleurnicher, fondre en larmes.*

BLUFF, adj. *brusque, rude.*

BLUSH, s. *rougeur,* f., *rouge,* m.; without a —, (99) *sans rougir,* or, *sans que le rouge lui monte au front;* (of innocence), *modestes rougeurs,* f. p.; no smile, no —, *on ne sourit pas, on ne rougit pas.*

BLUSH, v. *rougir* (at, *de*).

BOND, s. *traité,* m., *convention,* f., *contrat,* m.; a — of fraud, *un contrat frauduleux.*

BONNET, s. *chapeau,* m.

BOOK, s. *livre, registre,* m.

BOON, s. *bienfait,* m.

BOOR, s. *rustre,* m.

BOOT, v. *servir à;* what boots it? *à quoi sert-il?*

BOOTY, s. *butin,* m.

BORN, part. *né;* to be —, †*naître;* low —, *humble, d'humble descendance.*

BORROW, v. *emprunter* (from, *de*).

BOTH, adj. *tous les deux, l'un et l'autre.*

BOW, v. *saluer;* — by shame, *courber sous la honte.*

BOX, s. *boîte,* f.; snuff—, *tabatière,* f.

BOY, s. *garçon, enfant, petit garçon.*

BRAIN, s. *cerveau,* m., *tête,* f.; my — reels, *j'ai la tête en feu; la tête me tourne;* brainless, *sans cervelle.*

BRAVE, adj. *brave, vaillant, courageux.*

BRAVE, v. *braver.*

BRAVO, int. *bravo.*

BREAK, v. 1. *briser;* (heart), *se briser;* my heart will —, (49) *mon cœur se brise,* or, *va se briser ;* a breaking heart, *un cœur qui se brise ;* 2. (icc), *se briser, se désagréger* [1]; 3. (a cloud), *se dissiper, fondre ;* to — down, *se briser.*

BREAKFAST, s. *déjeuner,* m.

BREAST, s. *poitrine,* f., *sein,* m.

BREATH, s. *haleine,* f., *souffle,* m. ; to snatch from those lips one — of that fragrance, (88) *dérober,* or, *ravir une seule fois sur ces lèvres, ce parfum.*

BREATHE, v. *respirer.*

BREATHLESS, adj. *sans un souffle ;* — heavens, *cieux dans un silence profond,* or, *dont pas un souffle ne trouble le silence.*

BREEZE, s. *brise,* f. ; the night —, *la brise du soir, de la nuit.*

BRICKED, adj. *de briques ;* — floors, *planchers de briques.*

BRIDAL, adj. *nuptial ;* — home, *maison nuptiale ;* pl., bridals, *épousailles,* f. p.

BRIDE, s. (before marriage), *fiancée ;* (after), *épousée, jeune mariée, jeune femme.*

BRIDEGROOM, s. (before marriage), *fiancé ;* (after), *jeune marié.*

BRIGHT, adj. *brillant ;* — dreams, *rêves dorés.*

BRILLIANT, adj. *brillant.*

BRING, v. 1. (to carry), *porter, apporter ;* to — comfort, *apporter le confort ;* 2. (to lead in), *amener* [1] ; — ruin, *amener la ruine ;* — decay to ourselves, *amener,* or, *causer notre décadence.* 3. — in, *rapporter ;* — from, (71) *tirer de ;* — on, I have brought this on thee, (18) *c'est moi qui t'ai causé cette humiliation ;* — to, *porter à.*

BRONZED, adj. *bronzé.*

BROW, s. *front,* m.

BRUISE, s. *contusion, meurtrissure,* f.

BRUSH, s. (in paint.), *pinceau,* m.

BURN, v. *brûler.*

BURST, v. *éclater* (in, *en) ;* that burst their channels, (73) *qui débordèrent,* or, *qui brisèrent leurs impuissantes barrières.*

BURY, v. *enterrer, s'enterrer.*

BUSINESS, s. *affaire,* f. (in the general sense, use the plural *affaires);*

on particular —, *pour affaires privées.*

BUSTLING ABOUT, adj. *affairé ; allant et venant çà et là.*

BUT, conj. 1. *mais, toutefois ;* 2. (excepting), — one, *un seul excepté;* 3. (only), *ne . . . . que, seulement ;* — one quiver of that mocking lip, *un seul mouvement de cette lèvre moqueuse ;* — for the revolution, *sans la révolution ;* if he were — less proud, (93) *si seulement il était moins fier ;* 4. (if not), who should share it — Pauline? *qui le partagerait, si ce n'est P. ?*

BUY, v. 1. *acheter* [1] *(qch. à qqn.);* — the right to, *acheter le droit à,* 2. id., to — one's ransom, (71) *payer* [1] *sa rançon.*

BY, prep. 1. *par ;* 2. *à côté de, près de ;* by my side, (60) *à mes côtés ;* a palace by its lake, (60) *un palais sur le bord de son lac ;* 3. (in), *en ;* by coming, *en venant ;* by never showing, (34) *en ne montrant jamais ;* 4. id., by law, (75) *de par la loi ;* by-and-by, *à propos, tout-à-l'heure.*

BY-WORD, s. *fable,* f.

C.

CABBAGE, s. *chou,* m.

CALL, v. *appeler* [1] ; — on (visit), † *venir voir ;* call on us, *venez nous voir, venez à la maison ;* — on (to appeal to), *en appeler à ;* — up, *rappeler* [1], *faire revenir.*

CALM, s. *calme,* m. ; all —, *tout est calme, calme complet.*

CAN is translated by the Present Indicative of † *pouvoir ;* we can arrange, *nous pouvons arranger ;* who — it be that sends me those flowers? *qui peut bien m'envoyer ces fleurs ?* can we stay here? *pouvons nous nous arrêter ici ?* you — be proud, (35) *vous pouvez être fière ;* I cannot, *je ne puis pas ;* it cannot, it cannot be, (68) *cela ne se peut pas, cela n'est pas possible.* See COULD.

CANAILLE, s. *canaille,* f. ; I never notice such —, *je ne prends jamais garde à pareille canaille.*

CANCEL, v. *effacer* [1], *biffer.*
CANVAS, s. *toile,* f.
CAPITAL, adj. (excl.), *capital !
excellent ! délicieux !*
CAPITAL, s. (stock), *capital,* m. ;
(town), *capitale,* f.
CARE, s. *soin,* m., *souci,* m. ; to
take — of, † *prendre soin de.*
CARE, v. *s'occuper de, se soucier
de ;* I do not — a jot whether, (45)
*je me soucie comme de Colin-Tampon
si,* prov.
CAREFUL, adj. *soigneux.*
CARELESSLY, adv. *avec insou-
ciance, sans soin.*
CARRIAGE, s. *voiture,* f.
CARRY, v. 1. *porter ;* 2. (to lead),
conduire, amener (to, *à*) ; — home,
† *conduire chez soi ;* — off a prize,
gagner un prix.
CARTE, s. (fencing), *quarte,* f.
CASE, s. (med.), *cas,* m.
CASTLE, s. *château,* m. ; —s in
the air, (12) *châteaux en Espagne,*
prov.
CATCH, v. 1. *attraper ;* 2. † *séduire.*
CAVE, s. *cave,* f., *caveau,* m.,
mines, f. p., *souterrains,* m. p. ; caves
of knowledge, *les profondeurs de la
science,* or *du savoir.*
CEASE, v. *cesser,* † *prendre fin.*
CELEBRATED, adj. *fameux, célè-
bre.*
CELL, s. *cellule,* f.
CERTAIN, adj. *certain.*
CERTAINLY, adv. *certainement.*
CHAFE, v. *échauffer, irriter,*
† *mettre en colère.*
CHAIN, s. *chaine,* f.
CHAMBER, s. *chambre,* f.
CHAMELEON, s. *caméléon,* m.
CHANCE, v. *avoir la chance de ;
avoir lieu par chance,* or *par ha-
sard.*
CHANGE, s. *changement,* m.
CHANGE, v. *changer* [1] (with, *avec*).
CHANGEFUL, adj. *changeant,
amateur de changements.*
CHAOS, s. *chaos,* m.
CHARACTER, s. *bonnes mœurs,* f. p.
CHARMING, adj. and part. *char-
mant.*
CHEEK, s. *joue,* f.
CHEERED (to be), † *prendre
courage, être gai.*

CHERISH, v. *chérir.*
CHICKEN, s. *poulet,* m. ; roast —,
poulet rôti.
CHIDE, v. *murmurer, se* † *plain-
dre (de).*
CHILD, *enfant,* m. f. ; (excl.), —!
mon enfant !
CHILL, v. *glacer* [1], † *faire frisson-
ner.*
CHOICE, s. *choix,* m. ; to make
one's — out of, *choisir parmi,* † *faire
son choix parmi.*
CHOKE, v. *étouffer, suffoquer.*
CHOOSE, v. *choisir* (from out,
dans).
CHURL, s. *manant,* m.
CITIZEN, s. 1. *citoyen ;* 2. *roturier,
qui n'est pas noble.*
CITY, s. *ville, cité,* f.
CLAIM, s. *droit,* m., *prétention,* f.
CLASP, v. *enlacer* [1].
CLEAR, adj. *clair, limpide ;* a —
lake, *un lac limpide ;* it is as — as
a map, *c'est aussi clair que de l'eau
de roche,* prov.
CLERGYMAN, s. *ecclésiastique,
curé, prêtre ;* the — of the parish,
le curé de la paroisse.
CLERK, s. (of a merchant), *com-
mis ;* (of a lawyer), *clerc,* m.
CLEVER, adj. *fin.*
CLING, v. *s'accrocher à ;* (of per-
sons), — by, *s'attacher à, se presser
contre.*
CLOAK, s. *manteau,* m.
CLOCK, s. *'horloge,* f.
CLOSE, prep. *près de ;* — at hand,
tout près d'ici, à deux pas.
CLOSELY, adv. *de près.*
CLOTHES, s. *'habits,* m. p. ; (of a
baby), *braies, robes,* f. p.
CLOUD, s. *nuage,* m.
CLOUDLESS, adj. *sans nuages.*
CLOWN, s. *rustre, manant.*
Co., Cie. (abbr. for *compagnie,*
comm.).
COACH, s. *carrosse,* m. ; a — and
six, *un carrosse à six chevaux.*
COARSE, adj. *grossier ;* — viands,
aliments grossiers ; how — you are !
que vous êtes grossier !
COAST, s. *côte,* f. ; the — is clear,
*il n'y a personne sur la côte, il n'y a
plus d'encombre.*
COFFEE, s. *café,* m. ; to have some

—, †*prendre du café ;* — cup, *tasse à café,* f.

COIN, s. *pièce de monnaie,* f., *coin,* m.

COIN, v. (a story); I have a story —ed, *j'ai un conte frappé au bon coin,* or *bien imaginé.*

COLD, adj. and s. *froid ;* to be—, *avoir froid ;* it is —, *il fait froid.*

COLOR, s. *couleur,* f.

COME, v. 1. †*venir ;* I — to lay my fortune, (86) *je viens pour déposer ma fortune ;* (exclam.), come! *allons ! voyons ! —,* child, *allons, mon enfant ;* to — away, *s'en aller ;* come away, *allons-nous-en ;* to — down, *descendre ;* to — down-stairs, *descendre les escaliers ;* — home, *revenir au logis ;* — in, *entrer ;* — over, *revenir à ;* 2. (of things), *se faire, se produire ;* a great change came over M., *un grand changement se fit dans M.*

COMFORT, s. *confort,* m., *consolation,* f.; it is a great —, *cela réconforte beaucoup.*

COMFORT, v. *réconforter ;* be —ed, *consolez-vous.*

COMMAND, s. *commandement,* m., *ordres,* m. p., *commissions,* f. p.; to take the —, †*prendre le commandement ;* any —s? (57) *pas de commissions ?* heritage of —, (35) *héritage d'honneur.*

COMMANDER-IN-CHIEF, s. *commandant en chef.*

COMMON, adj. *commun.*

COMMON, s. *terrain communal,* m.

COMMONER, s. *homme de commun, vilain, non titré, sans naissance, qui n'est pas noble.*

COMO, s. *Côme,* m.; the lake of —, *le lac de Côme.*

COMPANION, s. *compagnon,* f. irreg. *compagne ;* traveling —, *compagnon* (or, *compagne*) *de voyage.*

COMPLETE, v. *achever¹,* *compléter¹.*

COMPLEXION, s. *teint,* m.

COMPLIMENTARY, adj. *flatteur,* -euse.

COMPROMISE, v. *compro†mettre.*

COMRADE, s. *camarade,* m., f.

CONCLUDE, v. †*conclure.*

CONDESCEND, v. *daigner, conde-* scendre à ; (ironic), you are very condescending, *c'est une grande faveur que vous nous faites.*

CONDESCENSION, s. *condescendance, bienveillance,* f.

CONDITION, s. *condition,* f.; (place), *situation,* f.

CONDOLE, v. (with), †*prendre part à la douleur de,* † *faire ses compliments de condoléance à* (on, *sur).*

CONDUCT, v. †*conduire ;* — to, *mener ¹ à.*

CONFER, v. *conférer¹;* which —s so much rapture, *qui cause tant de ravissement à ; qui transporte qqn. de joie.*

CONFESSION, s. *aveu,* m., *confession,* f.

CONFIDE, v. (in), *se confier à, avoir confiance en.*

CONFUSED, adj. *confus.*

CONFUSEDLY, adv. *d'une manière confuse, confusément.*

CONGRATULATE, v. *féliciter* (of, *de).*

CONNECTION, s. *parenté,* f.

CONQUER, v. †*vaincre.*

CONQUEROR, s. *conquérant, vainqueur,* m.

CONQUEST, s. *conquête,* f.; you complete your — over me, *vous achevez de faire ma conquête.*

CONSENT, s. *consentement,* m.

CONSENT, v. *con†sentir à.*

CONSIDER, v. *considérer¹,* remarquer.

CONSIDERATE, adj. *qui agit avec discrétion ;* so — in you, *c'est bien à vous,* id.

CONSOLE, v. *consoler* (*qqn. de qch.*).

CONSPIRATOR, s. *conspirateur,* -trice.

CONSTRUE, v. †*construire, com-* †*prendre.*

CONTRACT, s. *contrat,* m., *stipulation,* f.

CONTRADICT, v. *contre†dire à, s'opposer à ;* to — commands, *se* †*mettre en travers des ordres.*

CONTRAST, v. †*mettre en regard.*

CONVERSE, v. *converser.*

COOL, adj. *frais ;* of the coolest foliage, *du feuillage le plus frais.*

COOLNESS, s. *sangfroid*, m.

CORRECT, v. *corriger*[1].

COST, v. *coûter*.

COT, s. *maisonnette*, f.

COTTAGE, s. *chaumière*. (*Cottage*, m., in French, means a country residence.)

COULD, v. aux. †*pouvoir*.

Could is translated in French by the Conditional of *pouvoir*, and also by the Present, Imperfect, and Past indefinite of the Indicative mood, sometimes by the Subjunctive, according to its meaning in the sentence. The following illustrations will be a sufficient guide for the learner: Who could have sent me? *qui peut m'avoir envoyé?* what could have turned? (7) *qui peut bien avoir tourné?* that I could, *que ne puis-je;* could I see her, *si je pouvais la voir;* her love could forgive, *son amour pouvait* (or *pourrait*) *pardonner;* if the earth could swallow me, (49) *si la terre pouvait m'engloutir,* or, *puisse la terre m'engloutir;* what could thy letter contain? (18) *que pouvait bien contenir ta lettre?* how could they have learned? (60) *comment ont-ils pu savoir?* I could show, (18) *je pourrais montrer;* he could have married, *il aurait pu épouser;* couldst thou but see with my eyes, (36) *plût à Dieu que tu pusses voir avec mes yeux.*

COUNT, s. (herald.), *comte*, m. (fem. *comtesse*).

COUNTING-HOUSE, s. *caisse;* in the —, *à la caisse.*

COUNTRY, s. *pays*, m., *patrie, contrée*, f.; in the —, *à la campagne.*

COUPLE, s. *paire;* a — of dictionaries, (66) *une couple de dictionnaires.*

COURAGE, s. *cœur, courage*, m.; my — fails me, *le courage* (or, *le cœur*) *me manque.*

COURSE, s. (way of doing), *voie, manière d'agir*, f.; adv., of —, *naturellement.*

COURT, s. *cour*, f.

COVER, v. †*couvrir;* covered by, *caché par.*

COWARD, adj. *poltron, lâche.*

CRAWL, v. *se dérober en rampant* (from, *à*).

CREATE, v. *créer.*

CREDIT, s. *crédit*, m.

CRIMINAL, adj. *criminel.*

CROOK, s. (of a shepherd), *houlette*, f.

CROSS, v. *passer (à travers), traverser, croiser;* fencing-foils —ed over the mantel-piece, (11) *fleurets croisés* (or, *placés en croix*) *sur le manteau de la cheminée;* — but her path, (56) *sois seulement sur son chemin.*

CROWN, s. *couronne*, f.

CROWN, v. *couronner.*

CRUELTY, s. *cruauté*, f.

CRUMBLE, *s'effondrer, s'écrouler.*

CRUSH, v. *écraser, fouler aux pieds.*

CRY, v. *crier, s'écrier;* — in scorn, *s'écrier, le dédain aux lèvres.*

CURE, v. *guérir* (of, *de*).

CURIOSITY, s. *curiosité*, f.

CURIOUS, adj. *curieux.*

CURRENT, adv. *couramment;* to pass —, (42) *passer comme une lettre à la poste*, prov.

CURSE, s. *malédiction*, f. (on, *sur*).

CURSE, v. †*maudire;* cursed, *maudit;* curse away, *va toujours, maudis à ton aise;* curse his impertinence, *maudite soit son impertinence.*

CURTAIN, s. *rideau*, m.

CURTSY, *faire un salut, une révérence;* curtsies and turns away, *elle fait une profonde révérence et lui tourne le dos.*

CUSTOM, s. *coutume*, f., *convenances*, f. p., *habitude*, f.

CYPRESS, s. *cyprès*, m.

D.

DAILY, adj. *de jour;* — and nightly, *jour et nuit.*

DAMN, int.; — his readiness, *au diable sa présence d'esprit.*

DAMNABLE, adj. *maudit.*

DAMNABLY, adv. *diantrement.*

DAMSEL, s *damoiselle*, f. (*damoiselle* is obsolete, but exactly renders *damsel*).

DANCE, v. *danser;* dancing-master, *maître de danse.*

DANGER, s. *danger, péril,* m.

DARE, v. *oser* (governs an inf. without prep.); — I ask? *oserai-je demander?* I — say, *j'ose dire,* (used absolut.), *j'en rêponds.*

DARING, adj. *audacieux, téméraire, hardi.*

DARK, s. *obscurité,* f., *ténèbres,* f. p.; in the —, *dans les ténèbres, dans l'obscurité.*

DASH, v. *repousser, rejeter¹;* — to the ground, (57) *jeter qqch. à terre.*

DAUGHTER, s. *fille,* f.

DAY, s. *jour,* m., *journée,* f.; good day, *bonjour* (when meeting); *bonsoir, adieu, au revoir* (when parting); to-day, adv. *aujourd'hui;* this —, *aujourd'hui même;* daybreaking, s. *point du jour.*

DEAD, part. *mort* (past part. of †*mourir*), *défunt;* my — father, *mon père mort,* or, better, *défunt mon père* (*défunt* is placed before the possessive).

DEAF, adj. *sourd;* — to all but my passion, *sourd à tout excepté à la voix de la passion.*

DEAL, s. *quantité,* f.; a vast — of, *beaucoup de.*

DEAL, v. *trafiquer;* to — with, *traiter;* that we are to be thus dealt with, (17) *pour qu'on nous traite de cette façon;* — with, (57) *avoir affaire à, avoir noise avec.*

DEAR, adj. *cher* (before the noun); dearest, *mon très-cher, ma très-chère.*

DEATH, s. *mort,* f.; — to love, *mort pour l'amour, tombeau de l'amour;* (excl.), —! *morbleu!*

DECEIVE, v. *tromper;* to be —d, *se tromper.*

DECIDE, v. *décider, se décider.*

DECLINE, v. *décliner.*

DECOROUSLY, *dans le décorum;* — brought up, *élevé dans le décorum.*

DECREE, s. *décret,* m.

DEED, s. *action,* f., *fait d'armes,* m.

DEEM, v. *considérer, penser;* to — thus, *penser ainsi.*

DEEP, adj. *profond.*

DEEPLY, adv. *profondément.*

DEFENCELESS, adj. *sans défense.*

DEFENDER, s. *défenseur.*

DEFORMED, adj. *difforme.*

DEFRAUD, v. *dépouiller* (from, *de*).

DEJECTION, s. *affaissement,* m.

DELICIOUS, adj. *délicieux.*

DELIGHT, v. *se* †*plaire,* †*prendre plaisir* (in, *à*); —ed, *enchanté.*

DELIRIUM, s. *délire,* m.

DELIVER, v. *délivrer, débarrasser* (from, *de*).

DEMAND, v. *demander* (*à*), *exiger* (*de*).

DEMERIT, s. *démérite, peu de mérite.*

DENY, v. *décliner, refuser, dénier.*

DEPART, v. †*partir.*

DESCEND, v. *descendre.*

DESCRIBE, v. *d'*†*écrire.*

DESERT, s. (wilderness), *désert,* m.; (merit), *mérite,* m.

DESERT, v. *abandonner.*

DESERTION, s. *abandon, abandonnement,* m.

DESERVE, v. *mériter* (*de* before inf.).

DESHABILLE, s.; in —, *en deshabillé.*

DESIRE, v. *désirer* (governs inf. directly or preceded by *de;* also, the subj. See Rules, VIII.)

DESOLATE, adj. *désolé, désert, abandonné.*

DESPATCH, v. *se dépêcher.*

DESPISE, v. *mépriser.*

DESTRUCTION, s. *destruction,* f.; to smile — on brave hearts, *détruire en souriant de braves cœurs.*

DETAIL, s. *détail,* m.

DETECT, v. *dé*†*couvrir.*

DETHRONE, v. *détroner.*

DEUCE, *diantre* (fam.); and what the — do you know about, *et que diantre savez-vous de;* — take me, (8) *le diable m'emporte;* who the — could, (32) *qui diantre en viendrait à bout.*

DEVICE, s. *stratagème,* m.

DEVIL, s. *diable;* (excl.), the —! *au diantre!* what the —, *que diantre* (fam.).

DEVOTED, adj. *dévoué* (to, *à*).

DEVOTION, s. *dévouement.*
DIAMOND, s. *diamant*, m.
DICTIONARY, s. *dictionnaire*, m.
DIE, v. †*mourir.*
DIGNITY, s. *dignité*, f.
DINNER, s. *dîner, dîné*, m.
DIRECTORY, s. *Directoire*, m.
(See Rules, III.)
DISAPPOINTMENT, s. *désappointement*, m.
DISARM, v. *désarmer.*
DISCOVER, v. *dé †couvrir.*
DISCREDIT, v. *jeter du discrédit sur.*
DISDAIN, s. *dédain, mépris*, m.
DISDAIN, v. *dédaigner* (de bef. inf.).
DISDAINFULLY, adv. *d'un air dédaigneux.*
DISENCHANTED, adj. and part. ; to be —, *être désenchanté* (with, *de*).
DISGRACE, s. *honte*, f., *déshonneur*, m.
DISGRACE, v. *déshonorer.*
DISGUISE, s. *déguisement*, m. ; in —, *sous un déguisement.*
DISHONEST, adj. *malhonnête.*
DISHONORED, part. *déshonoré.*
DISOWN, v. *désavouer.*
DISTANCE, s. *distance*, f. ; in the —, *à distance ;* at a —, *à quelque distance.*
DISTANT, adj. *lointain ;* — land, *terre lointaine.*
DISTINCTION, s. (in the army), *grade*, m.
DISTRACTION! (excl.), *ô transport ! ô délire !*
DIVINE, adj. *divin.*
DIVINE, v. *deviner.*
DIVORCED, part. *divorcé* (from, *d'avec*).
DO, v. 1. †*faire ;* to — every thing in life, *tout faire dans la vie ;* to have to — with love, *avoir à faire avec l'amour ;* 2. *rendre ;* to — some service to, (64) *rendre quelque service à ;* to — homage, *rendre hommage ;* 3. to have done with, *en finir avec ;* you have done with me, (56) *vous n'avez plus rien à voir avec moi ;* 4. *réussir, faire l'affaire, être de saison, suffire ;* that won't do, (44) *cela n'est pas de saison, cela ne suffit pas ;* 5. (used

absol.), you renounce? I do, *vous renoncez ? J'y renonce ;* and if I did, *et si telle était mon intention ;* deuce take me if I do, (9) *le diable m'emporte si je vous comprends ;* do you? (52) *en vérité, vraiment ?* don't you? (51) *n'est-ce pas ?* (See Rules, VI.)
DOG, s. *chien ;* (idiom. and fam.), *animal, matois*, m. ; clever —, (32) *fin matois ;* sly —, *fin matois, rusé animal.*
DOGE, s. *doge*, m. ; the — of Venice, *le doge de Venise.*
DOGGEREL, s. *mesure ;* such —! *et quelle mesure !*
DOMESTIC, adj. *domestique, intérieur.*
DOOM, s. *destin*, m., *destinée*, f.
DOOR, s. *porte*, f. ; at the —, *à la porte.*
DOTE, v. *aimer éperdûment, extravaguer.*
DOUBT, s. *doute*, m. ; there is no — of that success, *cette chance ne fait pas doute.*
DOUBT, v. *douter.* (See Rules, VIII.)
DOWAGER, s. *douairière*, f.
DOWRY, s. (by the husband in favor of his wife), *douaire*, m. ; (by the parents), *dot*, f. : (thus, the play on words contained in section 49 cannot be well rendered in French ; M. Deschappelles means *douaire*, and Melnotte feigns to understand *dot*.)
DRAIN, v. *dépenser, épuiser ;* wealth —ed, *richesse épuisée ;* to — the cup to the dregs, (25) *épuiser* (or †*boire*) *le calice jusqu'à la lie.*
DRAW, v. *tirer ;* — aside (a curtain), *écarter ;* — out, *enlever[1] ;* to — out the pain, *enlever la souffrance ;* — oneself up (theatr.), *remonter la scène.*
DRAWER, s. *tireur ;* — of water, *porteur d'eau* (lit., carrier of water).
DREAD, v. †*craindre ;* to be —ed, *être à craindre.*
DREAM, s. *rêve, songe ;* (nightmare), *cauchemar*, m.
DREAM, v. *rêver* (of, *de*).
DREAMER, s. *rêveur, qui rêve.*
DRESS, s. *costume*, m., *habits*, m. pl., (of a lady), *robe*, f.

F   11

DRIVE, v. ; — mad, *rendre fou* (idiom.).

DRIVELLING, adj. *radoteur.*

DROP, s. *goutte*, f. ; drops, *gouttes de sueur ;* the — stand on your brow, (59) *la sueur perle sur votre front.*

DROP, v. 1. *laisser tomber ;* 2. *renoncer*[1] *(à) ;* to — an acquaintance, *renoncer à une connaissance.*

DRUDGE, v. *travailler dur.*

DUE, adj. *dû* (to, *à*).

DULL, adj. *stupide.*

DULY, adv. *dûment, comme il convient.*

DUMB, adj. *muet ;* are you struck —? (65) *êtes-vous devenu muet ?* — show, *par pantomime.*

DUNGEON, s. *donjon,* m.

DUPE, s. *dupe,* f.

DUPED, adj. and part. *dupé.*

DURING, prep. *pendant.*

DUTY, s. *devoir,* m.

E.

EACH, adj. *chaque ;* — one, *chacun.*

EAR, s. *oreille,* f.

EARTH, s. *terre,* f.

EASE, s. *facilité, aise,* f.

EASEL, s. *chevalet,* m.

EASILY, adv. *aisément ;* — done, *facile à faire.*

ECHO, s. *écho,* m.

ECONOMICAL, adj. *économe.*

EFFECT, s. *effet,* m.

EFFORT, s. *effort,* m. ; one — more, *encore un effort.*

EGG, s. *œuf,* m.

ELSE, adj. *autre, le reste ;* I forget all —, *j'oublie tout le reste ;* nothing —, (16) *rien autre, rien de plus.*

ELSE, adv. *autrement.*

ELSEWHERE, adv. *ailleurs.*

EMBITTER, v. *remplir d'amertume, empoisonner.*

EMBRACE, s. *étreinte,* f., *embrassement,* m.

EMPEROR, s. *empereur,* m.

EMPRESS, s. *impératrice,* f.

EMULATE, v. (36) *chercher à égaler.*

ENCHANTRESS, s. *enchanteresse,* f.

END, s. *but,* m., *fin,* f., *bout,* m. ; at journey's end, *au bout* (or, *à la fin*) *du voyage ;* at his fingers' ends, (45) *au bout de ses doigts.*

END, v. *finir.*

ENDURE, v. *endurer,* † *souffrir.*

ENEMY, s. and adj. *ennemi.*

ENERGY, s. *énergie,* f.

ENGAGE, v. *engager*[1] *;* (a servant, a clerk), † *prendre.*

ENGLISH, adj. *anglais ;* —man, s. *Anglais.*

ENJOY, v. *jouir (de).*

ENOUGH, prep. *assez ;* (before a noun), *assez de ;* (in French, *assez* precedes its regimen) to be base —, (50) *être assez bas.*

ENRICH, v. *enrichir.*

ENTER, v. *entrer ;* (theatr.), — Beauséant, *B. entre en scène ;* — Pauline from the inn, (59) *P. entre en scène, venant de l'auberge.*

ENTERTAINING, adj. *amusant, divertissant.*

ENTERTAINMENT, s. *amusement, divertissement,* m.

ENTHUSIAST, s. and adj. *enthousiaste.*

ENTRUST, v. *confier.*

ENVY, s. *envie,* f.

ENVY, v. *envier qqn., porter envie à qqn.*

EQUAL, adj. *égal.*

ERE, conj. *avant que* (subj.).

ERE, prep. *avant ;* — thy time, (69) *bien avant toi.*

ESCAPE, s. *échappatoire,* f. ; there is no — for you, (44) *il n'y a pas moyen que vous échappiez.*

ESCAPE, v. *échapper à.*

ESPECIALLY, adv. *spécialement, surtout.*

ESTATE, s. (condition), *état,* m., *condition,* f. ; (land), *propriété foncière.*

ETERNALLY, adv. *éternellement, pour jamais.*

EVEN, adv. *même ;* — Mr. Glavis, *même M. G. ;* — then, *même alors ;* not —, *pas même.*

EVENING, s. *soir,* m., *nuit,* f. ; — lodgment, *logement pour la nuit.*

EVENT, s. *événement,* m.

EVER, adv. (without neg.), *toujours ;* as —, *comme toujours ;*

(negat.), *à jamais ;* lost —more to me, *perdu à jamais pour moi.*

EVERGREEN, adj. *toujours vert, toujours verdoyant.*

EVERGREEN, s. *plante vivace, immortelle,* f.

EVERY, adj. *chaque ;* — day, *chaque jour ;* — one, *chacun, -une ;* every one who, *tous ceux qui ;* — thing, *tout, tout cela ;* with — wind, *avec le vent, avec chaque souffle du vent ;* —where, *partout.*

EVIDENTLY, adv. *évidemment.*

EXACTLY, adv. *exactement ;* — so, *justement.*

EXAMINE, v. *examiner.*

EXCEED, v. *surpasser.*

EXCEEDINGLY, adv. *extrêmement, beaucoup.*

EXCEL, v. *surpasser qqn., exceller à qch.*

EXCELLENCY, s. *excellence,* f.

EXCEPT, prep. *excepté.*

EXCESSIVELY, adv. *excessivement.*

EXCUSE, s. *excuse,* f. ; to be an —, † *servir d'excuse ;* the ladies are no longer your —, (44) *les dames ne vous servent plus d'excuse.*

EXCUSE, v. *excuser.*

EXECRATE, v. *exécrer.*

EXERTION, s. *action, activité,* f.

EXIT (Latin word used in theatr.), EXEUNT plur. of *exit.* Exit Madame Deschappelles into house, (34) *Madame Deschappelles sort,* or, *quitte la scène et rentre dans la maison ;* exeunt into house, (33) *ils quittent la scène et rentrent dans la maison.*

EXORCISE, v. *exorciser, chasser.*

EXPECT, v. *attendre, espérer*[1].

EXPENSES, s. *dépense,* f., *frais,* m. p.

EXPIRE, v. *expirer.*

EXPLORE, v. *explorer, chercher ;* —ing mind, *esprit chercheur.*

EXPOSURE, s. *découverte,* f., *éclat,* m. ; if the — should have chanced, *si par chance l'éclat avait eu lieu.*

EXPRESS, s. (messenger), *exprès,* m.

EXPRESSION, s. *expression,* f., *mot,* m.

EXTERIOR, adj. *extérieur.*

EXTRAVAGANT, adj. *prodigue, dépensier,* m.

EXULT, v. *se réjouir* (in, *de*) ; to — in the humiliation of, *triompher* (or, *se réjouir*) *de l'humiliation de.*

EYE, s. *œil,* pl. irreg. *yeux ;* I shall meet her —s, *mes yeux rencontreront les siens.*

F.

FACE, s. *figure, face,* f. ; his very —, *sa face elle-même ;* or never see my — again, (97) *ou je ne te reverrai jamais,* or, *ne te présente jamais devant mes yeux ;* before the — of man and heaven, *en présence des hommes et du ciel.*

FACE, v. *regarder en face.*

FACETIOUS, adj. *facétieux.*

FACT, s. *fait,* m. ; the — is, *le fait est que.*

FAIL, v. *manquer ;* my courage fails me, *le cœur me manque.*

FAINT, v. *s'évanouir, se trouver mal.*

FAIR, adj. *beau,* f. *belle (bel* instead of *beau* before a masculine noun commencing with a vowel or an *h* mute).

FAIR, s. *belle* (fem. of *beau*).

FAIRY, adj. *féerique.*

FAIRY, s. *fée,* f.

FAITH, s. *foi, fidélité,* f. ; (excl.), *ma foi !* sur mon honneur !

FAITHFUL, adj. *fidèle, dévoué ;* your most — servant, *votre très-dévoué serviteur.*

FAITHLESS, adj. *sans foi.*

FALL, s. *chute, décadence,* f.

FALL, v. *tomber, succomber ;* (blame), *tomber, retomber ;* pride has fallen, *l'orgueil a sombré,* or, *s'est abaissé ;* (morally), *tomber,* † *déchoir ;* angels have fallen, *des anges sont tombés,* or *ont déchu ;* (from, *de*), couldst thou — from power, (40) *tomberais-tu du faîte de la puissance.*

FALSE, adj. *faux* (fem. irreg. *fausse), infidèle ;* oh, false one ! *oh, trompeuse !* rumor is —, *la rumeur est fausse.*

FAME, s. *renommée*, f., *renom*, m., *gloire*, f.

FAMILY, s. *famille*, f.; — in trade, *famille dans le commerce*; one of our —, *un membre de notre famille*.

FAN, v. *éventer*; — oneself, *s'éventer*.

FANCY, v. *s'imaginer*; I — I see, *je m'imagine voir*.

FAR, adv. *loin*; it is not —, *ce n'est pas loin*; how — is it to, *quelle distance y a-t-il d'ici à*; so —, *jusque là*.

FARCE, s. *farce, comédie*, f.

FARE, v.; how —s it with you? *comment va?* (ellipt. and vulg.)

FAREWELL, interj. *adieu*.

FARTHER, adv. and adj. *éloigné*, *de plus*; life has no — ills, *la vie n'a plus de maux à m'offrir*.

FARTHING, s. *liard*, m.

FAST, adj. *vite, rapide*.

FAT, adj. *gras*, fem. *grasse*.

FATE, s. *destinée, sort*, m.

FATHER, s. *père*.

FATIGUED, adj. *fatigué*; — with laughter, — *de rire*.

FATIGUING, adj. and part. (adj. verbal), *fatigant*; (pres. part.), *fatiguant*.

FAVOR, s. *faveur*, f.

FAVORITE, s. and adj. *favori*, fem., *favorite*.

FEAR, s. *peur, crainte*, f.; for fear that, (23) *de crainte que*; to have — of, *avoir peur de*; we have no — of, *nous n'avons pas peur de*.

FEAR, v. †*craindre, avoir peur de, appréhender de*; don't — me, *n'appréhendez rien de moi*; never —, (33) *n'ayez crainte*.

FEAST, v. *fêter*.

FEED, v. *nourrir, se nourrir (de)*; to — on air, *se nourrir d'air, de vapeurs, de chimères*.

FEEL, v. †*sentir, se sentir*; I — more worthy thee, *je me sens plus digne de toi*.

FEELING, s. *sentiments*, m. pl.

FELLOW, s. (oftentimes is not translated in French), *camarade, compagnon*; (joc.), *gaillard, mortel*; my dear —, (3) *mon cher camarade*; the — imposed upon me, *le gars*

m'en a imposé; thou art a noble —, *tu es un brave garçon*; noble —! (50) *brave garçon!* low —s, *gens de basse extraction*; my — subject, (33) *féal sujet, mon camarade*.

FENCE, v. †*faire des armes, se livrer à l'escrime*.

FENCING, s. *armes*, fem. pl.; — master, *maître d'armes*.

FEVER, s. *fièvre*, f., *accès*, m.

FEVERISH, adj. *fiévreux*; your hand is —, (59) *votre main annonce la fièvre*.

FEW, adj. (*a few* followed by a noun), *quelques*, pl.; a — days, *quelques journées*; (small number), *peu de*; a few books, *quelques livres, peu de livres*.

FIDDLESTICK, s. *archet*, m. (fig. and fam.); foreign prince, foreign —, *prince étranger, blague étrangère*.

FIE, interj. *fi!*

FIELD, s. *champ*, m.; (of battle), *champ de bataille*.

FIEND, s. *démon*, m.; have —s a parent? *les démons ont-ils une mère?* —! *démon!*

FIERCE, adj. (of a man), *farouche*.

FIERY, adj. *brûlant, terrible*.

FIFTY, adj. num. *cinquante*.

FIGHT, v. *se †battre (avec)*, com-†*battre*.

FIGHTING, s. *l'action de se battre*; he understands — as well as he does Italian, (32) *il sait se battre aussi bien qu'il sait l'italien*.

FIGURE, s. *figure*, f.; he makes a very pretty —, *il fait assez bonne figure*.

FILL, v. *remplir*; to be —ed with, *être rempli de, être plein de*; — up, *remplir*.

FIND, v. *trouver*; to — some one a tool, (74) *trouver en quelqu'un un instrument*; to — out, *trouver, dé-*†*couvrir*.

FINE, adj. *fin, beau*; all very —, *tout cela est bien beau*.

FINGER, s. *doigt*, m.

FIRE, s. *feu*, m.

FIRM, adj. *ferme, solide*.

FIRST, adj. *premier, -ière*.

FIRST, adv. *d'abord, première-ment*; at —, *d'abord, au commencement*; at the —, *tout d'abord*.

FIT, adj. *convenable;* it is —, *il convient que, il est bon que* (subj.).

FIVE, num. *cinq.*

FLAME, s. *flamme,* f.

FLATTER, v. *flatter;* —ed, *flatté, qu'on flatte.*

FLESH, s. *chair,* f.; art thou — ? *es-tu en vie?*

FLOWER, s. *fleur,* f.; — pot, *pot de fleurs.*

FLY, v. *voler, s'envoler;* — back te, *s'envoler vers, re†prendre son vol vers;* (to run), *fuir.*

FOE, adj. *ennemi.*

FOIBLE, s. *faiblesse,* f., *faible,* m.

FOIL, s. (fencing), *fleuret,* m.

FOLD, v. (to one's heart), *presser sur son cœur.*

FOLIAGE, s. *feuillage,* m.

FOLKS, s. *gens,* m. pl.; great —, (12) *les grands.*

FOLLOW, v. †*suivre.*

FOLLY, s. *folie,* f.

FOND, adj. *amateur, qui aime;* not — of princes, *qui n'aime pas les princes.*

FONDLY, adv. *tendrement, avec tendresse.*

FOOL, adj. *fou, insensé;* a dull —, *un stupide lunatique;* to be a —, *être fou;* fool! *imbécile!*

FOOLED, part. *moqué.*

FOOLISH, adj. *fou;* — fellow, *jeune fou,* or, *vieux fou* (according to age).

FOOT, s. *pied,* m.; at the — of the Alps, *au pied des Alpes.*

FOR, conj. *car.*

FOR, prep. 1. *pour;* for this, for that, *pour cela;* for the same reason, *pour la même raison;* —ever, *pour jamais;* — myself, *quant à moi;* but — the revolution, *sans la révolution;* —years, *pendant des années;* 2. *depuis;* — the last six weeks, (14) *depuis six semaines,* or, *ces six dernières semaines;* — fear that, *de crainte que* (subj.).

FORBID, v. *repousser, défendre de.*

FORCE, v. *forcer* [1] (to, *à*).

FOREGO, v. *renoncer* [1] *à, abandonner, éloigner, se défendre de;* to — pride, (36) *se défendre de l'orgueil, abandonner tout orgueil.*

FOREIGN, adj. *étranger, -ère.*

FORESEE, v. †*prévoir;* I — it all, (15) *je prévois tout cela,* (fam.), *je vois tout cela d'ici.*

FORETELL, v. *pré†dire.*

FORGET, v. *oublier.*

FORGIVE, v. *pardonner (ych. à qqn.)* (for, *de*); to — for refusing, *pardonner d'avoir refusé;* forgotten, forgiven, *oublié, pardonné.*

FORGIVENESS, s. *pardon,* m.

FORLORN, adj. *abandonné;* idiom., — hope, *enfants perdus (d'une armée);* there shall not be a — hope without thee, (100) *il n'y aura pas à l'armée d'enfants perdus dont tu ne fasses partie.*

FORM, s. *forme,* f.; (of a woman), *formes,* fem. pl.

FORMALLY, adv. *formellement.*

FORSAKE, v. *abandonner, délaisser.*

FORSWORN, adj. *parjure,* m.; to be —, *se parjurer, être parjure.*

FORTHWITH, adv. *sur le champ, à l'instant.*

FORTUNATE, adj. *heureux, fortuné (de* before infinitive).

FORTUNE, s. *fortune, destinée,* f.

FOULLY, adv. *honteusement, d'une manière infâme.*

FOUNTAIN, s. *source, fontaine,* f.; low —, *humble source,* also, *source profonde.*

FOUR, num. *quatre.*

FRAGRANCE, s. *parfum,* m., *senteur,* f.

FRANTIC, adj. *insensé.*

FRAUD, s. *fraude,* f.; a bond of —, (76) *un contrat frauduleux.*

FREE, adj. *libre;* despair is —, (76) *le désespoir, c'est la liberté.*

FREEZE, v. *se glacer* [1] *; se figer* [1] *;* my blood —s in my veins, *mon sang se glace dans mes veines.*

FRENCH, adj. *français* [5]; Frenchman, *Français.*

FRIEND, adj. *ami.*

FRIENDLESS, adj. *sans amis.*

FRIENDSHIP, s. *amitié,* f.

FROM, prep. (provenance) *de;* (since), *dès, depuis;* — my first years, (69) *dès mes premières années;* — the date, *depuis la date;* from out a glossy bower, *du milieu d'une brillante charmille.*

FRUIT, s. *fruit*, m.

FUGITIVE, adj. *fugitif.*

FULFIL, v. *remplir, accomplir ;* could love — its prayers, (37) *si l'amour pouvait réaliser ses propres désirs,* or, *exaucer ses propres prières.*

FULFILMENT, s. *accomplissement,* m., *réalisation,* f.

FULL, adj. *plein ;* — bottom, *à large fond ;* a — bottom wig, *une perruque à la financière.*

FUNERAL, s. *enterrement,* m., *funérailles,* f. pl.

FURNITURE, s. *ameublement,* m., *meubles,* m. pl.

FUTURE, adj. *futur, avenir,* m. ; in the —, *dans l'avenir.*

G.

'GAD, int. *ah çà ! voyons !*

GAIN, v. *gagner ;* to — a step, †*faire un pas en avant,* or, fam., *avancer* [1] *d'un cran.*

GALE, s. *brise,* f., *vent,* m., *souffle de la brise.*

GALL, v. *blesser, être cuisant.*

GALLANT, adj. *brave ;* — old Damas, *le vieux brave Damas.*

GAOL, s. *prison, geôle,* f.

GAOLER, s. *geôlier,* m.

GARDEN, s. *jardin,* m.

GARDEN, v. *jardiner.*

GARDENER, s. *jardinier, -ière.*

GARISH, adj. *brillant, étincelant.*

GATHER, v. (round), *entourer.*

GAY, adj. *gai.*

GAZE, v. *regarder, jeter* [1] *un regard à,* or *sur.*

GENEROUS, adj. *généreux.*

GENTEEL, adj. *comme il faut ;* (of things), *bien porté.*

GENTLEMAN, s. 1. *un monsieur comme il faut ;* voc. gentlemen, *messieurs ;* to be a —, *être un homme comme il faut ;* 2. (nobleman), *gentilhomme* (pl. *gentilshommes*) ; a poor —, *un gentilhomme pauvre.*

GENTLY, adv. *doucement, gentiment.*

GENUS (corruption of *genius,* cannot be well translated in French) ;

he is only a —, (5) *ce n'est qu'un gêneux.*

GERMAN, s. and adj. *allemand.*

GESTURE, s. *geste,* m. ; to make a mocking —, (32) †*faire un geste moqueur.*

GET, v. *obtenir ;* — me a chair, *donnez-moi une chaise ;* to — in, *entrer, rentrer ;* to — out, †*prendre, aller chercher ;* to — over, *surmonter ;* I shall never — over it, *je n'en reviens pas,* or, *je ne m'accoutumerai jamais à l'idée,* id.

GIBBERISH, *baragouin, baragouinage,* m., *jargon,* m.

GIRL, s. *fille, jeune fille.*

GIVE, *donner,* †*faire présent de qch. à qqn. ;* I gave you revenge, *je vous ai donné votre revanche ;* — me your hand, Glavis, *votre main, Glavis* (ellipt.) ; to give birth, *donner le jour ;* to — back, *rendre.*

GLASS, s. *verre,* m.

GLASS, v. *refléter* [1], *se refléter,* thy image glassed in my soul, (71) *ton image reflétée dans mon âme.*

GLEAM, s. *lueur,* f. ; a — of sunshine, *une lueur d'en haut,* or, *un rayon de soleil.*

GLITTERING, s. *éclat,* m.

GLOAT, v. *dévorer des yeux.*

GLOOMY, adj. *triste, sombre.*

GLORIOUS, adj. *glorieux.*

GLORY, s. *gloire,* f.

GLOVE, s. *gant,* m.

GNAW, v. *ronger* [1].

GO, v. 1. †*aller* (the conj. *and* uniting *to go* to another verb is not translated in French, and the second verb is put in the infinitive) ; go *and* order the carriage, *allez donner ordre d'atteler ;* 2. (to leave), †*partir, s'en aller ;* are you not gone yet? *vous n'êtes pas encore parti ?* we will go hence, *nous allons nous en aller d'ici ;* 3. — out, †*sortir ;* go, *sortez !* 4. (disappear), *s'envoler, dis†paraître, s'éclipser ;* 5. — after, †*suivre qqn. ;* 6. — away, *s'en aller ;* 7. — back, *retourner, re*†*venir* (to, *à*) ; 8. — by, *se régler sur ;* 9. — in, *rentrer ;* 10. — on, *pour*†*suivre, continuer ;* (fam.), how go on the Deschap.? *id., comment va-t-on chez les Deschap.?* 11. — to, *aller vers, se diriger vers ;* to go to somebody, *aller trouver qqn., re†joindre, retrouver ;* 12. — up, (theatr.), *remonter la scène ;* 13. — with, *venir avec, aller avec.*

GOLD, s. *or,* m.

GOLDEN, adj. *d'or ;* the Golden Lion, (1) *le Lion d'or.*

GOOD, adj. *bon, excellent ;* very —, *très-bon ;* — looking, *beau garçon.*

GOOD, s. *bien, avantage ;* what — does it do to thee ? *quel avantage en retires-tu ?*

GOSSIP, s. 1. *cancan, caquet, commérage,* m. (are generally used in the plural) ; rustic —, *cancans villageois ;* 2. *conteur,* m., *commère,* f.

GOT (past part. of *to get*), *eu, eue ;* what have you —? *qu'avez-vous ?*

GRAMMAR, s. *grammaire,* f.

GRANDFATHER, *grandpère.*

GRANDILOQUENT, adj. *qui fait des phrases, phraseur ;* his Highness is —, *son Altesse fait des phrases.*

GRANT, v. *accorder ;* 2. (admit), *ad†mettre, re†connaître.*

GRATEFUL, adj. *reconnaissant.*

GRAVE, adj. *grâve ;* why so —? *pourquoi cet air grâve ?*

GRAVE, s. *tombe,* f., *tombeau,* m.

GRAVE, v. *graver.*

GREAT, adj. *grand, large ;* the —, *les grands ;* great-great-grandmother, *grand' grand' grand' mère* (See Rule I., ELISION.)

GREATNESS, s. *grandeur,* f.

GREEN, adj. *vert ;* (fig.), — with jealousy, *vert de jalousie.*

GREETING, s. *accueil,* m.

GRIEF, s. *désespoir,* m.

GRIEVOUSLY, adv. *grièvement.*

GROCER, s. *épicier,* m.

. GROUND, s. *terrain,* m. ; (fencing), take your —, *prenez du champ, en garde !*

GROW, v. 1. *grandir ;* 2. (with an adj.), *de†venir ;* thou art grown constant, *tu es devenu constant ;* to — more bold, *devenir plus audacieux ;* to — a torture, *devenir une torture ;* 3. — old, *vieillir, se faire vieux ;* to — lean, *maigrir ;* — fat, †*prendre de l'embonpoint ;* 4. id.,

on the canvas grew the life of beauty, (72) *sur la toile surgit* (or, *apparut*) *la beauté vivante ;* I grew thy adorer, (70) see ADORER.

GUARD, v. *garder, veiller sur.*

GUARDIANLESS, adj. *sans appui, sans protecteur.*

GUESS, v. *deviner, chercher à deviner.*

GUEST, s. *'hôte,* m.

GUILLOTINE, v. *guillotiner.*

GUILT, s. *culpabilité,* f., *crime,* m., *faute,* f. ; there is no guilt in the decrees of Providence, (99) *les décrets de la Providence ne nous rendent pas criminels,* or, *ne doivent pas nous être imputés à crime.*

GUILTILY, adv. *criminellement.*

GUILTY, adj. *coupable.*

GUITAR, s. *guitare,* f.

GUN, s. *fusil,* m.

GUSH (forth), v. *jaillir.*

H.

HA! *Ha !* —! he comes, *ha,* or, *mais le voici justement.*

HAIR, s. *cheveu,* m., *chevelure,* f.

HALF, adj. 1. *demi ; demi* qualifying a feminine noun remains invariable if placed before the noun ; *une demi-heure,* a half-hour; *une heure et demie,* half-past one ; 2. (followed by an adjective or a participle), *à moitié ;* — forgotten, *à moitié oublié.*

HALLOW, v. *sanctifier, rendre sacré ;* no image is —ed more from the rude hand of sacrilegious wrong, (75) *nulle image n'est plus sacrée,* or, *n'est plus à l'abri du grossier contact d'une main sacrilège et coupable ;* to be —ed, *être sanctifié, consacré par.*

HAND, s. 1. *main,* f. ; you had some — in that device, *vous avez eu un peu la main dans ce tripotage ;* 2. *signature,* f.

HAND, v. *re†mettre.*

HANDSOME, adj. *beau,* f. irreg. *belle.* (See FAIR.)

HANDSOMELY, adv. *d'une belle manière ;* — endowed, *richement doté.*

HANG, v. 1. *pendre;* — me, I will be —ed if, *je veux être pendu si;* — oneself, *se pendre;* 2. (fig.) *se suspendre;* I — upon the honey, (39) *je me suspends au miel.*

HAPPINESS, s. *bonheur,* m.

HAPPY, adj. *heureux, fortuné;* — to see, *heureux de voir;* to make somebody —, *rendre quelqu'un heureux,* or, †*faire le bonheur de qqn.*

HARD-WON, adj. *gagné avec effort;* — honor, *l'honneur si péniblement acquis.*

HARDEN, v. *endurcir, s'endurcir;* —ed, *endurci.*

HARE, s. *lièvre,* m.

HARK, interj. *écoutons;* — ye! *écoutez!*

HARMLESS, *inoffensif, qui ne peut faire du mal.*

HARSH, adj. *dur, bien dur;* a — word, *une parole dure.*

HASTE, s. *hâte,* f.; to make —, *se hâter, se dépêcher.*

HASTY, adj. *prompt, précipité, inconsidéré;* a — union, *une union précipitée, irréfléchie;* to be —, *se hâter, être prompt.*

HATCH, v. *couver, tramer, machiner.*

HATE, s. *haine,* f.; his love is —, *son amour, c'est de la haine.*

HATE, v. †*haïr.*

HATEFUL, adj. *odieux, digne de haine.*

HATRED, s. *haine,* f.

HAUGHTY, adj. *hautain.*

HAUNT, v. *hanter;* —ing eyes, *yeux qui vous suivent partout, qui vous obsèdent.*

HAVE, v. aux. 1. *avoir;* to — to say, *avoir à dire;* 2. id., I would— you come, *je voudrais que vous vinssiez;* and you would have a wife enjoy luxury, (98) *et vous voudriez qu'une femme vécût heureuse dans le luxe;* 3. †*faire;* as cloudless as I would have thy fate, (37) *aussi sans nuages que le sort que je voudrais te faire.*

HE, pers. pron. (subject to a verb expressed), *il;* (subject of a verb understood), *lui;* (bef. a conjunctive pronoun), *celui;* he is married, *il est marié;* when he was a boy,

quand il était encore un petit garçon; he is a stout fellow, is Claude, *c'est un gaillard solide que Claude;* I know he is, (32) *je sais qu'il l'est,* or, *que c'en est un;* who should he be, but? *qui serait-ce, sinon?*

HEAD, s. *tête, cervelle,* f.; their honest heads, *leurs 'honnêtes cervelles;* —strong, adj. *entêté, têtu.*

HEAR, v. 1. *entendre,* com-†*prendre;* 2. *écouter;* — me, *écoutez-moi;* 3. — of, *entendre parler de;* 4. — from, *apprendre de, entendre dire à;* what do I —? (47) *qu'est ce que j'apprends?*

HEART, s. *cœur,* m.; kind —, *bon cœur;* with all my —, (10) *de tout mon cœur;* so much at heart, (31) *tellement à cœur;* — ache, *peines de cœur,* f. pl.

HEARTH, s. *foyer,* m.; by the winter —, *l'hiver au coin du feu.*

HEARTLESS, adj. *sans cœur.*

HEAT, s. *chaleur,* f., *feu,* m. (same expression in the figurative sense, when speaking of passions).

HEAVEN, s. *ciel,* m.; (pl. irreg. *cieux*); excl. *ô ciel!* by —! *par le ciel!*

HEAVENLY, adj. *céleste.*

HEAVY, adj. *pesant, lourd;* — blow, *coup sensible.*

HEED, v. †*faire attention (à),* *écouter,* †*prendre garde à;* I heeded not, *je n'y pris pas garde,* or, *je n'y fis nulle attention.*

HEEL, s. *talon,* m.; to lay him by the heels, *se* †*mettre à ses trousses.*

HEIR, s. *'héritier, -ière;* — apparent to, *héritier présomptif de.*

HELP, s. *secours,* m.; —! (excl.) *au secours!*

HELP, v. *aider,* †*venir en aide à.*

HEM, int. *hem! euh!*

HENCE, adv. *d'ici, de là.*

HENCEFORTH, adv. *désormais* (may be put before or after the verb).

HERD, s. *troupeau,* m.

HERE, adv. *ici;* — and there, *çà et là;* — is, *voici;* — comes Mr. B., *voici M. B.;* —we are at Lyons, *nous voici à Lyon;* — there is no deceit, *ici il n'y a rien de trompeur;* — they are, (57-63) *les voici;* (the preceding examples show that *voici* precedes its regimen when it is a noun, and follows it when a pronoun; Ex., *voici Melnotte, le voici;* here is our revenge, (8) *voici notre revanche.*)

HERO, s. *héros,* m. (fem. irreg. *'héroïne*); in the masculine *héros* the *h* is aspirate; it is mute in the feminine *héroïne.*

HEWER, s. (of wood), *bucheron,* m.

HEY, int. *hé! hé!*

HIDE, v. *cacher.*

HIDEOUS, adj. *hideux.*

HIGH, adj. *haut* (generally before its noun), *élevé* (after it); —er birth, *naissance plus élevée;* — thoughts, *pensers sublimes, élevés.*

HIGHNESS, s. *Altesse,* f.; his or her —, *son Altesse;* — me no more, (57) *plus d'Altesse, s'il vous plaît; plus d'Altesse désormais.*

HILL, s. *montagne,* f., *côté, élévation de terrain.*

HIM, pers. pron. (direct object before the verb), *le;* (indirect object before the verb or regimen to a prep.), *lui;* I gave him to understand when I saw him, *je lui donnai à entendre quand je le vis;* they are taking him, etc., *c'est lui qu'on ramène en triomphe.* LUI! *et qui est ce monsieur* LUI?

HIRE, v. *louer les services de,* † *prendre à gages.*

HIS (her, its), 1. *son, sa, ses* (agree always in gender and number with the following noun, *i.e.* with the *possessed,* not with the *possessor* as in English); it is —, *c'est à lui, c'est le sien;* 2. (when speaking of parts of the body, the French use the article, *le, la, les,* not the possessive; Ex., about to take *her* hand, *sur le point de* LUI *prendre* LA *main* (lit. about to take to her the hand).

HIST, int. *chut!*

HIT, v. *frapper juste;* I have — it, *j'ai mon affaire, je tiens l'affaire,* fam., *j'ai mis le doigt dessus.*

HITHER, adv. *ici, par ici.*

HOLD, v. † *tenir;* to — life, *tenir la vie;* — me the slave, (32) *tenez-moi pour l'esclave; considérez-moi l'esclave;* —! *arrêtez! taisez-vous!*

pardon! un instant! (surprise), *tiens, tenez.*

HOLY, adj. *saint, sacré.*

HOMAGE, s. *' hommage,* m.; to do —, *rendre hommage.*

HOME, s. 1. *demeure,* f., *chez soi;* homeless, *qui n'a pas de chez soi;* what a —! *quel logis! quel résidence!* 2. *toit,* m. (lit. *roof*), *foyer* (lit. *hearth*); at —, to be —, *être à la maison;* to make a —, (70) *se bâtir une demeure, se faire son nid.*

HOMELINESS, s. (in furniture), *extrême simplicité.*

HOMELY, adj. *simple, commun.*

HONEST, adj. *' honnête;* an — man, (27) *un brave homme;* the — men, *les gens honnêtes;* poor but —, *pauvre mais honnête;* 2 (of things), *'honorable;* an — name, *un nom honorable.*

HONEY, s. *miel,* m.; —moon, *lune de miel.*

HONOR, s. *'honneur,* m.

HONOR, v. *' honorer;* to — somebody by, *faire l'honneur à qqn. de;* (inf.), — me by accepting it, *faites-moi l'honneur de l'accepter.*

HONORABLE, adj. † *honorable, qui a de l'honneur;* he is too — not to have revealed, (63) *il a trop d'honneur pour n'avoir pas révélé.*

HOPE, s. *espoir,* m., *espérance, f.*

HOPE, v. *espérer* 1; — on, — for, *espérer;* — for the laurel, *espérer le laurier.*

HORRID, adj. *'horrible.*

HORSE, s. *cheval,* m.

HOUR, s. *'heure,* f.; in the — of, *à l'heure de;* what is the —? *quelle heure est-il?* beyond the hour, (53) *au-delà de l'heure présente.*

HOUSE, s. *maison,* f. (when *house of* is understood in the English possessive case, translate it in French by the prep. *chez* before names of persons: Ex., to my mother's, *chez ma mère.*)

HOVEL, s. *baraque, f.*

HOW, adv. *comment* (is not translated after *to know,* in such sentences as, to know — to read, to write, to swim, etc., *savoir lire, écrire, nager*); when followed by an adjective in exclamations, translate it by *comme, que, combien :* how pale he is, (59) *comme il est pâle ;* — confused he looks, (65) *comme il paraît confus ;* — deep is woman's love, *combien profond est l'amour d'une femme,* or, *quelles profondes racines a l'amour,* etc. ; — fortunate I am, *que je suis heureux ;* — my heart swells within me, *comme mon cœur se dilate en moi ;* how forward these men are, *que ces hommes sont présomptueux ;* — you would have laughed, *que vous eussiez ri* (note the transpositions in the above sentences) ; idiom., in the sense of old tales : *comme quoi ;* how maidens have stooped, (70) *comme quoi des jeunes filles se sont abaissées.*

HOWEVER, adv. *quelque, si, tout ;* — lowly, *quelque humble,* or, *tout humble,* or, *si humble qu'il soit ; quel que* in two words before the verb *être,* and in that case *quel* agrees in gender and number with the following substantive ; Ex., however inexperienced, *quelle que soit son inexpérience ;* (absolut.), *néanmoins, cependant, toutefois.*

HUCKSTER, s. *revendeur ;* (in terms of contempt), *brocanteur, tripoteur.*

HUE, s. 1. *couleur, nuance,* f., *miroitements,* m. pl. ; the —s of glory, *les miroitements de la gloire ;* 2. *teinte,* f., *traits,* m. pl. ; your bronzed hues of time and toil, *vos traits bronzés par le temps et les fatigues.*

HUM, inter. *hon.*

HUMAN, adj. ' *humain, qui appartient à l'humanité ;* I am but —, *seulement, j'appartiens à l'humanité, je suis femme.*

HUMBLE, v. '*humilier.*

HUMBLY, adv. ' *humblement.*

HUMOR, s. ' *humeur, disposition d'esprit,* f. ; a better humor to you, *je vous souhaite une meilleure disposition d'esprit.*

HUMPBACKED, adj. *bossu.*

HUMPH, inter. *hum ! eh ! eh !*

HUNDRED, num. 1. *cent ;* when *cent* is preceded by a number, it is pluralized : five hundred louis, (29) *cinq cents louis ;* but it would remain

invariable if followed by another number ; two hundred and fifty louis, *deux cent cinquante louis.* The same rule applies to *vingt,* twenty. 2. (collective), *centaine,* f. ; a few — louis, *quelques centaines de louis ;* hundreds, *des centaines de gens.*

HURRAH, int. *hourra !*

HURRY, s. *hâte, précipitation,* f.

HUSBAND, s. *mari.*

HUSH, int. *silence, plus un seul mot.*

I.

I, pers. pron. *je, moi. Je* is used as the subject of a verb expressed ; *moi* stands as the subject of a verb understood or distant ; Ex., I do not doubt, *je ne doute pas ;* I, I doubt, *moi, je doute ;* I, the peasant born, *moi le paysan, né de paysans.*

ICE, s. *glace,* f.

IDEA, s. *idée,* f.

IDEAL, adj. *idéal ;* — charms, (72) *un charme idéal (idéal* is not used in the plural).

IDLE, adj. *paresseux ;* id., it were — to reproach, *ce serait perdre son temps que de faire des reproches.*

IDOL, s. *idole,* f.

If, conj. *si.* The use of *si* implies two propositions. The verb following *si* states the *condition ;* the other verb, expressed or understood, shows what event *will* or *would* follow. RULE : *If the verb expressing the event contemplated is in the future, the verb following* SI *is put in the* PRESENT *Indicative ; if the same verb be in the* CONDITIONAL, *the verb governed by* SI *is put in the* IMPERFECT *Indicative.* The following sentence (15) will illustrate both cases : If she but hear thee, Claude, she *will* (or *would*) love thee, *si seulement elle* T'ENTEND *causer, elle* T'AIMERA, or, *si seulement elle* T'ENTENDAIT *causer, elle* T'AIMERAIT. Sometimes the present is used instead of the future, for emphasis' sake ; Ex., a mere mocking gesture, and you *are* a dead man, *un simple geste moqueur, et vous* ÊTES *un homme mort (si vous*

faites is understood at the beginning of the sentence).
ILL, adj. *mal.*
ILLUSTRIOUS, adj. *illustre.*
IMMEDIATELY, adv. *immédiatement, sans délai.*
IMMORTAL, adj. *immortel;* to become —, (39) *de†venir immortel,* or, poet., *se re†vêtir d'immortalité.*
IMPOSE, v. *en imposer* (upon, *à*).
IMPOSTOR, adj. *imposteur.*
IMPROVE, v. *embellir;* †*faire valoir, s'améliorer;* that improves the air, *cela fait valoir la tournure.*
IMPUDENT, adj. *impudent;* a monstrous— person, *un personnage terriblement impudent.*
IN, prep. 1. *dans;* in action, (34) *dans l'action;* in a man, *dans l'homme;* in it, in them, *dedans;* you never care what is in them, (26) *vous ne vous occupez jamais de ce qu'il y a dedans (dedans* is an adverb, it cannot have a regimen). 2. *à, en* (the substantive following *en* takes no article), to throw into prison, *jeter¹ en prison;* to be in danger, *être en danger;* in Lyons, *à Lyon;* in the moment of, *au moment de;* in the eyes of God, *aux yeux de Dieu;* in the hour of shame, *à l'heure de la honte;* in a shooting-match, *à un tir;* 4. *de;* colonel in the French army, *colonel de l'armée française;* other countries in Europe, *d'autres contrées de l'Europe;* a lesson in parsing, (44) *une leçon d'analyse grammaticale;* 5. (after a superlative), *de;* the truest fellow in the world, (9) *le plus sûr gaillard du monde;* the gayest bachelor in Lyons, (1) *le célibataire le plus gai de Lyon;* the richest girl in the province, *la plus riche héritière du pays,* 6. id., in this short absence, *pendant cette courte absence;* in sleep, *pendant le sommeil, en songe.*
INCENTIVE, s. *stimulant, encouragement,* m.
INCH, s. *pouce,* m.; I know the path, nay, every — of it, *je connais le sentier, que dis-je, pas un pouce de ce sentier ne m'est inconnu.*
INDEED, adv. *en vérité, vraiment.*

INDELICACY, s. *manque de délicatesse,* m.
INDUCE, v. *engager¹* (to, *à*); she will be —ed to marry, (43) *on⁹ l'engagera à épouser.*
INDUSTRY, s. *industrie,* f.
INEXPERIENCED, adj. *inexpérimenté.*
INEXPRESSIBLES, s. pl., *inexpressibles,* m.
INFORM, v. *ap†prendre à qqn., informer qqn.*
INJURE, v. *faire du mal à, outrager¹, blesser;* to be grievously —ed, *recevoir une cruelle injure.*
INN, s. *auberge,* f.
INQUIRE, v. *s'informer.*
INQUISITIVE, adj. *curieux.*
INSCRIBE, v. †*inscrire;* your name was —d upon it, *votre nom y était inscrit.*
INSECT, s. *insecte,* m.; — (butterfly), *papillon,* m.
INSPECT, v. *inspecter, jeter les yeux sur.*
INSPIRE, v. *inspirer;* to inspire somebody with a proper ambition, *inspirer à qqn. une ambition convenable;* those —ing toils, (71) *ces travaux inspirés, ces œuvres inspirées.*
INSTANT, s. *moment, instant,* m.
INSTANTLY, adv. *à l'instant, à la minute.*
INSUFFERABLE, adj. *insupportable.*
INSULT, s. *insulte,* f.
INSULT, v. *insulter;* 2. (to neglect one's duty, to be wanting in respect towards persons or things), *insulter à;* to — her agony, *insulter à son agonie.*
INTEND, v. *avoir l'intention* (to, *de);* if my daughter were intended to marry, *si ma fille était destinée à épouser,* id.
INTEREST, s. *intérêt,* m.
INTERESTING, adj. *intéressant* (from, *par*).
INTERFERE, v. (in), *inter†venir* (dans), *se mêler (de).*
INTERIOR, s. *intérieur,* m.
INTERRUPT, v. *inter†rompre.*
INTIMATE, adj. *intime.*
INTO, prep. *dans* (see IN).

INTRODUCE, v. (in the sense of presentation) *présenter à qqn.*

INVENTION, s. *invention;* (trick), *stratagème,* m.

INVEST, v. 1. *investir;* 2. (money), *placer*[1]; to — a property, *faire le placement de.*

INVIOLATE, adj. *sans tache.*

INVITE, v. *inviter,* †*faire des avances.*

IRON, s. *fer,* m.; — fortune, *destinée de fer.*

IT, pers. pron. *il, elle,* nom.; *le, la,* acc. referring to a precedent substantive; *ce, cela,* referring to no particular noun; (*ce* is used before the tenses of the verb *être*), it is the one, *c'est celui,* or, *celle;* to submit to it, *se soumettre à cela* (see to BE, ₰ 5).

ITALIAN, s. and adj. *italien, d'Italie;* — campaign, *la campagne d'Italie.*

J.

JACKANAPES, s. *âne, singe, fat,* m.

JANET, s. pr. *Jeannette.*

JEER, s. *raillerie, moquerie;* to be the — of every tongue, (68) *être l'objet des plaisanteries de toutes les langues.*

JEST, s. *plaisanterie,* f.

JEST, v. *plaisanter.*

JEWEL, s. *bijou,* m., *joyaux,* f. pl.

JOIN, v. *re†joindre,* †*aller rejoindre.*

JOINTURE, s. *douaire,* m.

JOKE, s. *plaisanterie,* f.

JOT, s. *brin,* m.; I don't care a — whether, (45) *je me soucie comme de Colin-tampon si,* idiom.

JOURNEY, s. *voyage,* m.

JOVE, int.; by Jove, *par Jupiter.*

JOY, s. *joie,* f.; — (excl.), *ô joie!* give me —, (12) *félicitez-moi;* I wish you —, *je vous présente mes félicitations.*

JOYFUL, adj. *joyeux.*

JUDAS, s. pr. *Judas* (*s* silent in pron.).

JUGGLE, s. *tours de passe-passe, escamotage,* m.

JUGGLE, v. †*faire des tours de passe-passe, escamoter.*

JUNO, s. pr. *Junon,* f.

JUST, adj. *juste, bon.*

JUST, adv. *justement* (is often rendered in French by the verb †*venir de,* expressing a past just elapsed); he has just won, *il vient de gagner;* read this letter just received from my friend, (47) *lisez cette lettre que je viens de recevoir de mon ami;* I will just step in, *je vais justement entrer,* or, *je ne fais qu'entrer;* — as, *de même que, comme, de la même manière que.*

JUSTICE, s. *justice,* f.; to do —, (76) †*faire justice, rendre justice à.*

K.

KEEP, v. 1. †*tenir, se tenir;* to — an oath, *tenir un serment;* to — up one's dignity, *main†tenir sa dignité;* — his rank, *maintenir son rang;* to — up (a building), *entretenir.*

KILL, v. *tuer;* — me, *tue-moi;* — her, *tue-la.*

KIND, adj. *bon, aimable.*

KING, s. *roi.*

KNAVE, s. *coquin, fripon.*

KNEE, s. *genou,* m.

KNOCK, s. *coup;* (theatr.), — at the door, *on frappe à la porte.*

KNOCK, v. *frapper;* — together, *s'entrechoquer.*

KNOW, v. 1. (a thing), †*savoir,* †*connaître;* know, Glavis, *sachez, Glavis;* now I know it, *je le sais maintenant;* (a path), *connaître (un sentier);* 2. (a person), *connaître;* — by sight, (8) *connaître de vue.*

KNOWLEDGE, s. *science,* f., *savoir,* m.

L.

LACKEY, s. *laquais,* m.; from — to —, *de laquais en laquais.*

LAD, s. *garçon, jeune homme,* fam. *gars;* lads, *jeunes gens, gars, camarades.*

LADY, s. *dame;* the ladies, *les dames;* voc. *madame,* pl. *mesdames;* young — (newly married), *jeune dame, jeune mariée.*

LAKE, s. *lac,* m.

LAMP, s. *lampe*, f.
LANDLORD, s. *propriétaire*, m. f.;
— (of an inn), *aubergiste*, m. f.
LANGUAGE, s. *langue*, f., *langage*, m.
LANGUIDLY, adv. *languissamment, d'un air langoureux.*
LARDER, s. *office, garde-manger*, m.
LARGE, adj. *grand* s; — sum of money, *forte somme;* — sacrifice, (9) *large, fort sacrifice.*
LAST, adj. *dernier, -ière;* —night, *hier au soir.*
LAST, adv. *en dernier lieu;* at —, *enfin, à la fin;* to the —, (24) *jusqu'au bout;* to the —, (70) *jusqu'à la fin, jusqu'au dernier jour;* for the — six months, (14) *depuis six semaines.*
LATE, adv. *tard;* it is —, *il est tard;* so —, *si tard;* too —, *trop tard;* it is not too —, *il est encore temps.*
LATTICE, s. *treillage, treillis*, m.; (door), *porte en treillis*, or, *à claire-voie.*
LAUGH, v. †*rire, se moquer de, plaisanter;* id., to — the wrong side of one's mouth, *rire à l'envers.*
LAUGHTER, s. *rire*, m.
LAUREL, s. *laurier*, m.
LAVISH, v. *prodiguer.*
LAW, s. *loi*, f.
LAWFUL, adj. *légal;* to accept the — hand, (87) *accepter légalement la main.*
LAY, v. 1. *placer* 1, †*mettre, poser, déposer;* to — rights, *déposer des droits, abdiquer;* — hand upon, *poser sa main sur, mettre la main sur;* 2. *coucher, étendre.*
LEAD, v. †*conduire;* — in, *amener* 1, *conduire;* — back, *ramener* 1 *à;* — on, *guider, conduire.*
LEAGUE, s. *lieue*, f.
LEAGUE, v. *se liguer, agir de concert* (with, *avec*).
LEAN, adj. *maigre.*
LEARN, v. ap†*prendre* (*à* bef. inf.), *savoir.*
LEAST, adj. *moindre;* adv. *moins;* at —, *au moins, à tout le moins.*
LEATHER, s. *cuir*, m.
LEAVE, v. *laisser, abandonner,*

quitter; — us, *laissez-nous;* I don't like leaving, (34) *je n'aime pas à laisser.*
LEFT, adj. *gauche;* to the —, *à gauche.*
LEFT, p. p. *laissé;* (with a negat.), we have no noblemen left, *nous n'avons plus de nobles;* (affirm.), we have still noblemen —, *nous avons encore des nobles;* there is nobility still —, *il y a encore, il reste encore une noblesse;* it is the only course — to thee, (80) *c'est la seule voie qui te reste;* to be — to, *rester à.*
LEGACY, s. *legs*, m.
LEND, v. *prêter.*
LENGTH; at —, *à la fin* (loc. adv.).
LESS, adv. *moins;* it is no — a person than, (8) *ce n'est rien moins que*, id.
LESSON, s. *leçon*, f.
LEST, conj. *que* (subj.); I tremble lest he be discovered, (24) *je tremble qu'il ne soit découvert.*
LET, v. 1. *laisser;* — him enter, *qu'il entre, faites-le entrer;* — me introduce to you, *permettez-moi de vous présenter;* 2. (LET is often rendered in French by the Imperative of the next verb), let us escape, *échappons-nous;* — it pass, (74) *passons là-dessus;* let me come to, (74) *venons à*, or, *laisse-moi arriver à;* — me hope, *espérons*, or, *laissez-moi espérer;* — me see, *que je voie*, or (absolut.) *voyons;* 3. (followed by a noun is translated by the 3d pers. subj.); — the blame fall, *que le blâme retombe;* let it not chafe thee, (60) *que cela ne t'irrite pas;* — the marriage take place, (48) *que le mariage ait lieu;* 4. to let somebody into a secret, †*mettre qqn. au courant d'un secret;* — out, *lâcher, donner libre carrière à.*
LETTER, s. *lettre*, f.
LETTERED, adj. *imprimé.*
LEVEL, v. *niveler* 1, †*mettre sur le même niveau, abaisser;* — a pistol, *élever* 1 *un pistolet en visant.*
LIAR, s. *menteur, -euse.*
LIFE, s. *vie*, f.
LIFT, v. *lever* 1, *élever* 1; who dared to — his eyes to thee, (40)

qui osa élever ses regards jusqu'à toi; to — to eternal summer, (38) *élever dans un été sans fin.*

LIGHT, s. *lumière,* f.

LIGHT, v. *éclairer.*

LIKE, adj. *semblable à, ressemblant à;* to be like somebody, *ressembler à quelqu'un;* to be — a representative, (35) *être comme un représentant, ressembler à un représentant.*

LIKE, conj. (as), *comme.*

LIKE, v. 1. *aimer;* 2. *trouver, se trouver;* how do you — that ring? (30) *comment trouvez-vous cette bague,* or, *que dites-vous de cette bague?* how does Pauline like her new dignity? *comment P. se trouve-t-elle de sa nouvelle dignité?* 3. When followed in English either by an Infinitive or a present participle, it takes in French the preposition *à* and the following verb is put in the present of the Infinitive. Ex., I should like to see, *j'aimerais à voir;* I don't like leaving girls, (34) *je n'aime pas à laisser les jeunes filles;* I don't like doing business, (51) *je n'aime pas à faire les affaires.*

LIKENESS, s. *portrait,* m., *ressemblance,* f.

LIMB, s. *membre,* m.

LINE, s. (in writing), *ligne,* f.; — of business, *genre* (m.) *d'affaires, industrie,* f.; (poetry), *vers,* m.

LIP, s. *lèvre,* f.

LISTEN, v. *écouter.*

LITTLE, adj. 1. (small size), *petit;* 2. adv. (small quantity), *peu de;* a — coffee, *un peu de café.*

LIVE, v. †*vivre;* — again, re- †*vivre;* long —the Prince! *vive le Prince!*

LIVING, pres. part. and adj. *vivant, animé.*

LOATHSOME, adj. *honteux, dégoûtant.*

LODGE, v. *loger¹.*

LODGMENT, s. *logement,* m.

LONELINESS, s. *isolement,* m.; — of habits, *habitudes d'isolement.*

LONG, adj. *long.*

LONG, adv. *longtemps;* — since, *depuis longtemps;* to be — gone, *être longtemps absent.*

LONG, v. *désirer ardemment,* the heart that longed to show its .dol, (73) *le cœur qui soupirait après le moment où il pourrait montrer à son idole.*

LOOK, s. *regard, coup d'œil,* m.; a — of insult, *un regard insultant.*

LOOK, v. 1. (to look, to look at), *regarder, jeter¹ les yeux sur;* — down, *regarder en bas;* — in, *regarder à l'intérieur;* — in the face, *regarder en face;* — into, *regarder au fond de;* — round, *regarder de tous côtés;* — on, *regarder, avoir les yeux* (or, *les regards) fixés sur;* — up, *lever¹ les yeux, élever ses regards;* — over, *par|courir des yeux;* — higher, *porter ses regards plus haut, viser plus haut, avoir de plus hautes visées;* — to somebody (for marriage), *songer à, avoir l'œil sur, jeter¹ son dévolu sur;* 2. (to appear), *avoir l'air de,* †*paraître, sembler, avoir l'apparence de;* that looks very neat, (63) *tout cela paraît soigné, propre;* how lovely she looks, *quelle mine séduisante elle a;* 3. (to resemble), - - like, *ressembler à, paraître;* 4. - out, †*prendre garde;* — you, *voyez-vous, prenez garde.*

LORD, s. and int. *seigneur,* m., my lord, *milord;* my kind --, *mon doux seigneur.*

LOSE, v. †*perdre;* — not a moment, *ne perds pas un moment;* lost, *perdu, déchu;* he is lost, *il est perdu.*

LOT, s. *destinée,* f.

LOUIS, s. *Louis,* m.; Louis the Fourteenth, *Louis quatorze.* (In speaking of the order of sequence of monarchs, the French use no article, and they use the cardinal instead of the ordinal number.)

LOVE, s. 1. *amour,* m.; to be in — with, *être épris de, tomber amoureux de, s'amouracher, s'éprendre de;* a woman in — with herself, *une femme amoureuse d'elle-même;* 2. (word of endearment), sweet —, *douce amie.*

LOVE, v. *aimer.*

LOVELY, adj. *digne d'être aimé, charmant, séduisant.*

LOVER, s. *amant, amoureux.*

LOW, adj. *bas;* — birth, *basse naissance;* — born, *de basse extraction;* as — as, *aussi bas que.*

LOWLY, adj. *humble, pauvre.*

LOYAL, adj. *loyal, féal* (*féal* is obsolete).

LUCKY, adj. *heureux, favorisé du sort;* (fam.), *chançard, qui a de la chance;* a — man, *un heureux mortel;* it is — that, *il est heureux que* (subj.).

LURE, v. *attirer, leurrer,* †*séduire;* — on to, *attirer vers.*

LUSTRE, s. *lustre, éclat,* m., *rayons,* m. pl.

LUTE, s. *luth,* m.; sweet —, *luth enchanteur.*

LUXURY, s. *luxe,* m.

LYONNESE, adj. *lyonnais.*

LYONS, s. pr. *Lyon,* m.

M.

MA'AM, *Mâme* (familiar abbreviation for *Madame,* used only by servants).

MAD, adj. *fou,* fem. irreg. *folle;* (before a masc. noun beginning with a vowel or an *h* mute, the masculine form *fol* is used instead of *fou*), *insensé.* Some called me —, *certains* (or *d'autres*) *m'accusaient de folie;* are you —? *avez-vous perdu l'esprit?* a —hour, *une heure folle,* or, *une heure de folie;* madhouse, *maison de fous,* f., *asile d'aliénés,* m.

MADDEN, v. *rendre fou,* †*mettre en rage.*

MADNESS, s. *folie,* f.

MAGIC, s. *talisman, secret magique,* m.

MAGISTRATE, s. *magistrat,* m.

MAID, s. *servante, domestique;* (children's nurse), *bonne;* lady's —, *femme de chambre.*

MAIDEN, adj. *fille, de jeune fille.*

MAKE, v. 1. †*faire;* to — somebody pass as, (9) *faire passer quelqu'un pour;* remorse has made me a new being, *le remords a fait de moi un autre être;* to — disdain, *faire dédaigner;* 2. *faire, rendre, devenir;* to — happy, *rendre*

heureux; to —sacred, *rendre sacré;* to — ruin less appalling, *rendre la perte moins terrible;* thou wouldst be only made more dear, (41) *tu ne me serais devenu que plus cher;* to be made a torture, *devenir une torture;* to make void and null, *déclarer nul et de nul effet;* 3. (followed by a double accusative), it made my whole soul a chaos, (73) *cela fit de mon âme entière un chaos.*

MAN, s. '*homme* (when connected with an adjective or another noun, *man* is not translated in French, and the adjective or noun is used substantively); of another —, *d'un autre;* old —, *vieillard;* man! (int.), *mon brave!* a lucky —, *un heureux mortel.*

MANNER, s. *manière, façon d'agir,* f.

MANTEL-PIECE, s. *cheminée,* f., *manteau de la cheminée.*

MANTLE, s. *manteau,* m.

MANTLE, v. to — somebody, *couvrir quelqu'un d'un manteau.*

MANUFACTURER, s. *fabricant, manufacturier,* m.

MANY, adj. 1. *plusieurs,* pl. of both genders; so — triumphs, *tant de triomphes;* many a, *plus d'un, beaucoup de;* many a foreign prince, *plus d'un prince étranger,* or, *bien des princes étrangers.*

MAP, s. *carte,* f.; (prov.), it is as clear as a map, (9) *c'est aussi clair que de l'eau de roche.*

MAR, v. *troubler.*

MARBLE, adj. *de marbre.*

MARBLE, s. *marbre,* m.

MARBLED, adj. *de marbre.*

MARGIN, v. *border, entourer.*

MARIAN, s. *Marianne,* f.

MARK, s. *marque,* f.

MARK, v. *marquer.*

MARRIAGE, s. *mariage,* m.

MARRY, v. *se marier avec, épouser qqn., marier;* she will — Mr. Beauseant, *elle se mariera avec M. B.,* or, *elle épousera M. B.;* I will not — her, *je ne l'épouserai pas;* to — the Adriatic, *épouser l'Adriatique;* Mr. Deschap. will marry his daughter to, *M. D. mariera sa fille à* (or *avec*).

From the above examples, it is seen that *marier*, actively, has for its subject the person who gives his or her consent, or performs the ceremony; *se marier avec*, reflect., has for its subject and object the contracting parties. *Se marier avec* is much more used than *épouser;* and this latter is not well used in the passive form. Ex., this day they shall be married, *aujourd'hui ils seront mariés* (not *épousés*).

MARSEILLES, s. *Marseille*, f.

MASTER, s. *maître, professeur,* m.; fencing —, dancing —, music —, *maître* or *professeur d'escrime, de danse, de musique.*

MASTER, v. *dominer, maîtriser.*

MATCH, s. (marriage), *parti,* m.; he is no — for Pauline, *ce n'est pas le parti qui convient à P.,* or, *il n'est pas ce qu'il faut pour P.*

MAY, v. 1. *May* expressing *possibility* is generally rendered by the present of the Indicative of †*pouvoir, je puis* or *je peux, tu peux,* etc.; you — bait the horses, (1) *vous pouvez faire rafraîchir les chevaux;* may I, *puis-je;* they — talk, *on peut parler,* or, *on peut dire tout ce qu'on voudra de;* you — read, *vous pouvez lire;* we — be all generals, (46) *nous pouvons tous devenir généraux;* 2. (expressing a doubt), *il est possible que* (subj.), *peut-être;* she — forget, (15) *il est possible qu'elle oublie,* or, *peut-être oubliera-t-elle;* may-be, *peut-être;* there — be hope, *il y a peut-être encore de l'espoir;* they — have forced her, *ils l'ont peut-être forcée.*

ME, pron. *me, moi, à moi; me* before the verb is accusative or dative; *moi* is used instead of *me* after the verb, when in the Imperative affirmative; *moi* is used as regimen to prepositions. Ex., for me, *pour moi;* with me, *avec moi.*

MEAN, adj. *bas, méprisable, mesquin, humble;* the meanest, *les plus humbles;* — looking, *grossier, rustre.*

MEAN, v. 1. †*vouloir dire, signifier;* what can it —? *qu'est-ce que tout cela veut dire,* or *signifie?* 2.

— for, *destiner à;* the lady the letter was meant for, (17) *la dame à qui la lettre était destinée.*

MEANS, *moyens,* m. pl.

MEANWHILE, adv. *en attendant.*

MEET, adj. *propre à;* more — for your reception, *plus propre à vous recevoir.*

MEET, v. (with), *rencontrer;* to — on the road, *rencontrer en chemin;* — in heaven, *se re†voir au ciel;* — demands (in business), *parer à des demandes;* how shall I — him? *comment soutiendrai-je sa vue?* well met I (excl.), *bonne rencontre!*

MELANCHOLY, s. *mélancolie,* f.

MEMBER, s. *membre,* m.; silent —, *un membre muet, qui n'apparaît pas.*

MEMORY, s. *mémoire,* f., *souvenir,* m.; (poetical, but obsolete), *souvenance,* f.

MENIAL, adj.; her — ruffians, *ses bandits de domestiques.*

MERCANTILE, adj. *mercantile;* to be —, (50) *avoir l'esprit mercantile,* or, *les idées mercantiles.*

MERCHANT, s. *marchand, négociant,* m.

MERCIFUL, adj. *miséricordieux.*

MERCY, s. 1. *pitié, miséricorde,* f.; 2. *merci, discrétion,* f.; at your —, (1) *à votre merci,* or, *à votre discrétion;* for —'s sake, *par grâce.*

MERIT, s. *mérite,* m.

MERRY, adj. *joyeux;* to make —, *faire bombance, choyer*[1].

MESSENGER, s. *messager, -ère.*

METHINKS, v. *il me semble;* methought, *il me semblait* (unipers.) *que* (Indicative).

MEXICO, s. *le Méxique,* m. (takes the definite art.).

MIDNIGHT, s. *minuit,* m.; a — student o'er the dreams of sages, (72) *à minuit, studieux songeur, absorbé par les rêves des sages;* — (adj.) *de minuit.*

MIDST, s. *milieu;* in the — of, *au milieu de;* from the — of, *du milieu de.*

MIGHT, v. 1. is generally translated by the Condit. of †*pouvoir, je pourrais,* etc.; that — be, *cela pourrait être,* or, *c'était peut-être;*

we — give, *nous pourrions donner;*
he — not have written, *il n'aurait pu écrire;* 2. *Might* is sometimes rendered by the Subjunctive :
that they — learn, (20) *qu'ils puis-
sent* (or *pussent*) *apprendre.*

MILK, s. *lait,* m.

MILORD, s. *milord.*

MIND, s. *esprit,* m.

MIND, v. *s'occuper de,* †*faire
attention à;* don't — him, *ne fais
pas attention à lui,* or, *ne t'occupe
pas de lui.*

MINE, adj. poss. *le mien, la
mienne;* this is —, (16) *c'est le mien,*
or, *la mienne;* the fault was —,
c'était ma faute, or, *la faute en est à
moi.*

MINGLED IN, p. p. *mêlé à, pris
dans, enveloppé dans.*

MIRACLE, s. *miracle,* m.; to succeed to a —, (23) *réussir à merveille,
à miracle; avoir une réussite prodi-
gieuse.*

MIRE, s. *boue,* f.

MISCHIEF, s. *malice,* f.; to make
—, *faire des siennes,* id.

MISER, s. *avare,* m.

MISERABLE, adj. *misérable.*

MISERY, s. *malheur,* m., *misère,
infortune,* f.

MISS, v. *manquer;* I missed him
(turn in French, *he missed to me*), *il
m'a manqué.*

MIST, s. *nuage,* m., *brume,* f.

MISTAKE, v. (somebody), *se
mé†prendre sur le compte de qqn.;*
you — me, *vous vous méprenez sur
mon compte.*

MISTAKEN, part. *trompé;* to be
—, *se tromper.*

MOCKERY, s. *moquerie, raillerie,*
f.; it is no —, *ce n'est pas une moquerie, une plaisanterie.*

MOCKING, adj. *moqueur, -euse*
(after the noun).

MOMENT, s. *moment,* m.; in the
— of, *au moment de.*

MONEY, s. *argent,* m.

MONSTROUS, adj. *monstrueux.*

MOON, s. *lune,* f.

MORE, adv. 1. *plus;* no —, *ne . . .
plus;* (still), *encore;* one word —,
encore un mot; one stage —, (54)
encore une étape; 2. no —, *plus,*

plus *désormais, rien de plus;* he
does not garden any —, *il ne jar-
dine plus;* 3. (at the end of a sentence), *davantage;* 4. (exclam.),
bien plus, encore.

MORN, s. *matin,* m.

MORNING, s. 1. *matin,* m.; good
—, *bonjour;* a very good —, *bien
le bonjour;* 2. (space of time before
noon), *matinée,* f.; all the —, *toute
la matinée.*

MORROW, *le lendemain matin;*
good —, *bonjour;* to —, *demain.*

MOST, MOSTLY, adv. *le plus,
très;* — obedient, *très-obéissant.*

MOTHER, s. *mère;* voc. *mère!*
ma *mère!* — to a princess, *mère
d'une princesse.*

MOULD, s. *moule,* m.; that sole
alloy of thy most lovely —, (69) *ce
seul alliage dans l'or divin dont tu
es formée.*

MOUNTEBANK, s. *saltimbanque,
bateleur, matamore.*

MOURN, v. *pleurer sur qqn., porter le deuil de qqn.*

MOURNER, s. *qui est en deuil;*
—'s prayers, *les prières du deuil.*

MOUTH, s. *bouche,* f.

MOVE, s. *mouvement,* m.; to
make a —, (90) *faire un mouvement.*

MOVE, v. 1. é†*mouvoir;* moved,
ému.

MUCH, adv. *beaucoup, autant;* as
— coolness as, *autant de sangfroid
que;* I cannot say as — for, *je ne
puis en dire autant de.*

MURMUR, v. *murmurer.*

MURMUR, s. *murmure,* m.

MUSIC, s. *musique;* — master,
maître de musique.

MUSICAL, adj. *musical;* — with
birds, (38) *plein d'oiseaux mélo-
dieux, plein du ramage des oiseaux.*

MUST, v. is translated in French
by the Present Indicative of †*devoir,
je dois,* etc., or by the unipersonal
verb *il faut;* in the latter case, the
subject of *must* becomes the indirect
object of *il faut;* Ex., you must
marry her, (42) *vous devez l'épouser,*
or, *il vous faut l'épouser,* or, *il faut
que vous l'épousiez;* she — have
loved him well, (63) *il faut qu'elle*

l'ait bien aimé; we — make haste, *nous devons nous hâter,* or, *il faut nous hâter;* you — allow me, *vous me permettrez;* you — have divined, *vous devez avoir deviné;* I — wish you good morning, *il me faut vous souhaiter le bonjour,* or, *il me faut prendre congé de vous;* it — not be, *cela ne doit pas être,* or, *il ne faut pas que cela soit;* you — be a man, *vous devez montrer que vous êtes un homme.*

MUTE, adj. *muet;* a —, *un muet.*

MY, poss. *mon, ma, mes* (see Rules on Euphony, Chapter I. 3). In speaking of parts of the body, the French use the definite article *le, la, les,* instead of the possessive, when there is no possible mistake as to the person. Ex., I lift my eyes to Pauline, *je lève les yeux vers P.*

MY LADY, s. *milady,* f.

MYRTLE, s. *myrte,* m.

MYSELF, pron. pers. *moi-même,* m. f.

MYSTERIOUS, adj. *mystérieux.*

MYSTERY, s. *mystère,* m.

N.

NAME, s. *nom,* m.

NAME, v. *nommer.*

NATIVE, adj. *natal.*

NATURE, s. *nature,* f.; peasant's —, *écorce du paysan.*

NAY, adv. 1. *non, que dis-je;* 2. (affirm.), *oui, vraiment, soit.*

NEAR, prep. *près de;* (adv.), *près, tout près.*

NEAT, adj. *propre, soigné.*

NECESSARY, adj. *nécessaire.*

NEED, v. *avoir besoin de, falloir;* I don't —, *je n'ai pas besoin;* we only — your signature, *nous n'avons plus besoin que de votre signature,* or, better, *il ne nous faut plus que votre signature;* it would —, *il faudrait.*

NEVER, adv. *jamais; ne . . . jamais;* — more, *jamais plus.*

NEW, adj. (other), *nouveau, autre;* (newly made), *neuf,* fem. irreg. *neuve.*

NICHED, adj. *placé dans une niche;* a saint — in cathedral's aisles, (75) *un saint niché dans les ailes d'une cathédrale.*

NIGHT, s. *nuit,* f., *soir,* m. f.; to —, *cette nuit,* or, *ce soir;* last —, *hier soir, la nuit dernière, à la soirée d'hier;* — is past, *la nuit a fait place au jour;* daily and nightly, *jour et nuit.*

NINE, num. *neuf.*

NO, 1. adv. *non;* 2. adj. indef. *aucun, nul;* it is no less than, *ce n'est rien moins que.*

NOBILITY, s. *noblesse,* f.

NOBLEMAN, s. *noble,* m.

NOBLY, adv. *noblement.*

NONE, pron. *personne (personne* as an indefinite pronoun is masculine; but *personne* meaning a person is feminine).

NONSENSE, s. *absurdité,* f.

NOON, s. *midi,* m.; at —, *à l'heure de midi.*

NOR, adv. *ni;* nor I, (4) *ni moi non plus.*

NORTH, s. *nord,* m.

NOT, adv. 1. *ne* before the verb, and *pas* or *point* after it. Ex., I do not construe affronts, *je ne relève pas un affront.* If the verb is understood, use *pas* alone. Ex., not I, *pas moi;* not here, *pas ici;* not at all, *pas du tout;* not a moment is to be wasted, (48) *pas un moment à perdre;* not one farthing, *pas un liard;* why not? *pourquoi pas?*

NOTARY, s. *notaire,* m.

NOTE, s. 1. (letter), *note,* f., *lettre,* f., *billet,* m.; 2. (commerce), *billet,* m.

NOTHING, adv. *rien; ne . . . . rien;* he thought of nothing else, (83) *il ne pensait à rien autre,* or, *vous étiez son unique penser.*

NOTICE, v. †*prendre garde à, remarquer.*

NOTWITHSTANDING, adv. *en dépit de tout.*

NOUN, s. *nom,* m.; the — substantive, *le nom substantif.*

NOURISH, v. *nourrir.*

NOW, adv. *maintenant;* —a-days, *de nos jours.*

NURSE, v. (a thought), *caresser une pensée, s'arrêter à une pensée.*

O.

OAK, s. *chêne*, m.
OAKEN, adj. *de chêne*.
OATH, s. *serment*, m.
OBEY, v. *obéir* (*à*).
OBJECT, s. *objet*, m.
OBLIGE, v. *obliger*[2].
OBLIVION, s. *oubli*, m.
OBSERVE, v. *remarquer, s'apercevoir* (that, *que*).
O'CLOCK, at two o'clock precisely, *à deux heures, heure militaire*.
ODOR, s. *parfum*, m.
OF, prep. *de*.
OFF, adv. well —, *à son aise*.
OFFENCE, s. *offense*, f.
OFFER, s. 1. *offre*. f. ; 2. (in marriage), *demande en mariage*.
OFFER, v. †*offrir*.
OFFICER, s. *officier*, m.
OH, int. *oh !* but —! *mais, hélas !*
OLD, adj. 1. *vieux*, fem. irreg. *vieille* (there is another masculine form, *vieil*, used before a vowel or an *h* mute) ; — man, *vieillard ;* — woman (vocat.), *la vieille ;* 2. (in rank), *ancien, vieux*.
ON, prep. 1. (upon), *sur ;* 2. — all sides, *de tous côtés ;* — your wedding-day, (57) *pour le jour de vos noces*, or simply, *le jour de vos noces*. *On* in comp. may be rendered by the verb *continuer*, or the adverb *toujours ;* go on, *allez toujours ;* I still toiled on, *je continuai à travailler avec ardeur*.
ONCE, adv. 1. *une fois ;* — more, *une fois encore ;* at —, *à l'instant, sur le champ, immédiatement, de ce pas, du coup, tout d'un coup ;* 2. (formerly), *jadis ;* — loved, *jadis aimé*.
ONE, num. 1. *un ;* — of these days, *un de ces jours ;* — o'clock, *une heure ;* (taken absolutely requires the use of *en*), to accept one offer, to refuse another, *accepter une offre*, EN *refuser une autre ;* to take a lesson or give —, (33) *prendre une leçon ou* EN *donner une ;* 2. (a single), — kiss, *un seul baiser ;* 3. (a person), *quelqu'un ;* one I can trust, (58) *quelqu'un de*

sûr, or, *qqn. à qui je puisse me fier ;* with — who owes his position, (35) *avec quelqu'un qui doit sa position ;* 4. (with a relative pronoun), *celui, celle*, etc. ; of — who, *de celui qui ;* the —, *celui, celle ;* 5. (idiom.), one's servants are so vain, (60) *nos domestiques ont tant de vanité*, or, *on a des domestiques si vains ;* 6. (omitted after an adjective), oh, false one ! *oh ! trompeuse ;* the false —, *la trompeuse, l'infidèle ;* fair —, (61) *ma belle*.
ONLY, adj. *seul, unique ;* — daughter, *fille unique*.
ONLY, adv. *seulement, ne . . . . . que*.
OPEN, v. † *ouvrir ;* part. *ouvert ;* in — street, *en pleine rue*.
OPPORTUNITY, s. *occasion*, f.
OR, conj. *ou*.
ORANGE, s. *orange ;* — grove, (39) *bosquet d'orangers*.
ORDER, v. *ordonner, donner des ordres* (*à*); to — horses to one's carriage, (67) *donner ordre d'atteler*, or, *de mettre les chevaux à la voiture*.
OTHER, adj. *autre ;* wise judges are we of each other, (53) *que nous sommes bons juges l'un de l'autre*.
OUGHT, is translated by the conditional of † *devoir ;* you — to be, *vous devriez être ;* we — not to be selfish, (49) *nous ne devrions pas être égoïstes ;* he — to be one, (63) *il devrait en être un ;* he — to have been the Grand Turk, *il aurait dû naître le grand Turc*.
OUR, pron. poss. *notre*, plur. *nos*, m. f.
OUT, adj. 1. *dehors ;* 2. — of (by means of), *au moyen de, grâce à, par ;* — of malice, *par malice ;* 3. nine times — of ten, *neuf fois sur dix*.
OUTBID, v. *surenchérir* (*sur qqn.*).
OUTCAST, s. *exilé, proscrit, un homme mis hors la loi*.
OUTRAGE, v. *outrager ;* — the laws, *braver les lois*.
OUTSHINE, *éclipser*.
OVER, 1. prep. *sur, au dessus de, par dessus ;* — his shoulder, (60)

par dessus son épaule; 2. (adv.) all —, *partout;* to be —, *être fini, achevé;* all is —, *tout est fini, tout est dit;* it is all —, *c'est fini, c'en est fait;* it was all — with them, (23) *tout fut fini, bâclé avec elles.*

OVERSHADOW, v. *ombrager,* †*couvrir de son ombre.*

OVERTAXED, adj. *surtaxé,* fam. (33) *refait.*

OWN, adj. *propre;* I was ·my — lord, (71) *je devins mon propre maître;* of my —, of your —, *en propre;* my — dear love, (37) *o mon bien-aimé, bien* À MOI; (*own* is not translated when not followed by a noun), my — property, *mon propre bien;* as if it were their —, (31) *comme si c'était le leur.*

OWN, v. *admettre;* it must be owned, *il faut admettre.*

P.

PACIFY, v. *pacifier.*

PAIN, s. *peine, douleur,* f.

PAINT, v. †*pcindre;* (depict), *dé†peindre.*

PAINTER, s. *peintre,* m.

PAIR, s. *paire,* f.

PALACE, s. *palais,* m.

PALE, adj. *pâle.*

PALLID, adj. *pâle;* — with despair, *pâle de désespoir.*

PAPER, s. *papier,* m.

PARDON, s. *pardon,* m.; you will beg my —, (57) *vous implorerez mon pardon;* (with *demander* the possessive becomes the indirect object of the verb), *vous* ME *demanderez pardon.*

PARENT, s. *parent,* m. (father), *père.*

PARENTAL, adj. *des parents.*

PARISH, s. *paroisse,* f.

PARSING, s. *analyse grammaticale,* f.; a lesson in —, (44) *une leçon d'analyse.*

PART, s. *part,* f., *parti,* m.; to take part with, (47) *prendre le parti de;* parts, *contrées,* f. pl.; in these parts, *dans ces contrées.*

PART, v. *se séparer* (from, *de*); I cannot — from thee, *je ne puis me séparer de toi.*

PARTLY, adv. *en partie.*

PARTY, s. *partie,* f., *parti,* m.; — of pleasure, *partie de plaisir.*

PASS, v. *passer;* — an ordeal, *traverser,* or, *subir une épreuve;* to make somebody pass off as, *faire passer quelqu'un pour.*

PASSION, s. *passion;* there is a — in, *il y a toute une passion dans.*

PASSIONATE, adj. *passionné, ardent, plein de feu.*

PAST, s. *passé,* m.; the — was hers, *le passé lui appartenait.*

PATIENCE, s. *patience,* f.; I have no — with you, (95) *vous me faites perdre patience,* or, *vous me mettez hors des gonds.*

PATRON, s. *protecteur,* fem. *protectrice.*

PATRONIZE, v. *patronner.*

PAUSE, s. *pause,* f.; (theatr.), *après un instant de silence.*

PAUSE, v. *s'arrêter.*

PEACE, s. *paix,* f.; (excl.), *silence! paix!*

PEASANT, s. *paysan,* m.

PEDIGREE, s. *lignage,* m.

PEEP, v. *regarder à la dérobée.*

PENSIONER, s. *pensionnaire.*

PEOPLE, s. *gens,* m. plur.; where are our —? *où sont nos gens?* cabbages better than other people's, (5) *choux meilleurs que ceux des autres.*

PERFECT, adj. *parfait, véritable;* to be in a — fever, (3) *être dans une véritable fièvre.*

PERFUME, v. *parfumer.*

PERHAPS, adv. *peut-être.*

PERJURE, v. *se parjurer;* then thou art —d, (42) *alors tu te parjures,* or, *tu deviens parjure.*

PERMIT, v. *per†mettre.*

PERSON, s. *personne,* f.

PERSUADED, part.; to be —, *se laisser gagner, se laisser persuader.*

PHILOSOPHY, s. *philosophie,* f.

PICTURE, s. 1. *tableau,* m., *peinture, toile,* f.; 2. (description), *peinture, esquisse;* dost thou like the —? (39) *aimes-tu l'esquisse?*

PILLOWED (to be), *reposer, avoir pour oreiller.*

PISTOL, s. *pistolet,* m.

PITEOUSLY, adv. *piteusement;* most —, *le plus piteusement du monde, de la manière la plus piteuse.*
PITIFUL, adj. *digne de pitié.*
PITY, s. 1. *pitié,* f.; to have — on, (66) *avoir pitié de;* 2. *pitié,* f., *dommage,* m. ; what a —, *quel dommage!*
PLACE, s. *lieu,* m., *place,* f., *endroit,* m.; to take —, (48) *avoir lieu.*
PLACE, v. *placer* ¹.
PLAN, v. †*faire le plan de;* (a garden), *dessiner (un jardin).*
PLANK, s. *planche,* f.; of (safety), *planche de salut.*
PLANT, v. *planter.*
PLAY, v. 1. *jouer;* — on the guitar, *jouer de la guitare;* 2. (to pretend), *jouer, faire;* to — the miser, *jouer le rôle d'un avare.*
PLAYER, s. *comédien;* strolling --, *comédien ambulant.*
PLEASANT, adj. *agréable.*
PLEASE, v. †*plaire (à);* if it — you, *si cela vous plaît;* if you —, *s'il vous plaît;* if he had pleased it, (82) *si cela lui avait plu.*
PLEASURE, s. *plaisir,* m.
PLENTIFULLY, adv. *abondamment.*
PLOT, s. *trame,* f., *complot,* m.
PLOUGHSHARE. s, *soc de la charrue.*
PLUCK, v. *tirer par.*
POCKET, s. *poche,* f.; — book, *carnet de poche.*
POESY, s. *poésie,* f.
POETRY. s. *poésie,* f.
POINT, v. — to, *indiquer, montrer du doigt.*
POMP. s. *pompe,* f.
POMPOUS, adj. *pompeux.*
POOH, int. *ah bah!*
POOR, adj. *pauvre.*
POORLY, adv. *pauvrement, faiblement.*
PORTER, s. *portier (-ière), concierge,* m. f.
PORTFOLIO, s. *portefeuille,* m.
PORTMANTEAU, s. *porte-manteau,* m.
POSITION, s. *place, position,* f.
POSTERITY, s. *postérité,* f.
POUR, v. 1. *répandre, verser;* to

— prayers, *répandre, verser des prières (versez des larmes avec des prières;* BOSSUET); 2. *épancher, exhaler;* to — into song, (73) *exhaler en un chant d'amour;* to — one's worship into poetry, (14) *épancher son amour en vers.*
POVERTY, s. *pauvreté,* f.
POWER, s. *pouvoir,* m., *puissance,* f.; to have — upon, (69) *avoir pouvoir sur, pré†valoir sur, l'emporter sur.*
POWERLESS, adj. *sans force, sans pouvoir, impuissant.*
PRACTICE, v. *pratiquer.*
PRAY, v. *prier, supplier, demander dans les prières;* (absolutely), *je vous en prie, s'il vous plaît.*
PRECISELY, adv. *précisément;* (precise hour), *heure militaire.*
PREFER, v. *préférer* ¹.
PREFERENCE, s. *préférence,* f.
PREPARE, v. *préparer, se préparer;* to be —ed, *être préparé à;* be prepared, *sois prêt.*
PRESENT, s. *présent,* m.; at —, *à présent;* adj. *présent, actuel.*
PRESENTLY, adv. *tout à l'heure.*
PRESUMING, adj. *présomptueux;* a — fellow, *un jeune présomptueux.*
PRETEND, v. 1. †*faire semblant de;* to — not to hear, (30) *faire semblant de ne pas entendre;* 2. — to, *prétendre à.*
PRETENSION, s. *prétention,* f.
PRETTY, adj. *joli.*
PRICELESS, adj. *sans prix, qui n'a pas de prix.*
PRIDE. s. *fierté,* f., *orgueil,* m.; the — of my heart, *l'orgueil de mon cœur,* or, *de mon âme;* love and —, *amour et amour-propre.*
PRIEST, s. *prêtre,* m.
PRINCESS, s. *princesse,* f.
PRIOR, adj. *antérieur.*
PRISONER, s. *prisonnier, -ière.*
PRIZE, s. *prix.*
PROCEED, v. 1. (to go on), *continuer;* 2. (to go to), *se rendre à.*
PROCEEDING, s. *procédure,* f., *poursuites,* f. pl.
PROFESSOR, s. *professeur.*
PROMISE, v. *pro†mettre, s'en-gager* ¹ (to, *à*).

PROMISING, adj. *qui promet;* a — youth, (7) *voilà un jeune gaillard qui promet.*

PROMOTION, s. *promotion,* f.; (in rank), *avancement,* m.

PRONOUNCE, v. *prononcer*[1]; not as you — it, *pas comme vous le prononcez.*

PROOF, s. *preuve, marque,* f.

PROPER, adj. *propre, convenable.*

PROPERTY, s. *bien,* m., *propriété,* f.

PROPHET, s. *prophète,* m.

PROPOSE, v. *proposer;* †*faire une demande en mariage;* to make him —, (9) *lui faire faire une demande en mariage.*

PROSPERITY, s. *prospérité,* f.

PROTECTOR, s. *protecteur,* m. (*-trice*).

PROUD, adj. *fier, orgueilleux.*

PROVERB, s. *proverbe,* m.

PROXY, s. *fondé de pouvoirs, mandataire;* by —, (50) *par procureur.*

PRUDISH, adj. *prude.*

PSHAW, int., *bah! fi!*

PULL, v. *tirer.*

PUNISHMENT, s. *punition,* f.

PURCHASE, s. *achat,* m., *emplette,* f.

PURE, adj. *pure.*

PURPOSE, s. *objet;* for the —, (9) *pour cet objet.*

PURSE, s. *bourse,* f.

PUSH, v. *pousser;* — aside, *pousser qqn. de côté;* — to, *pousser vers.*

PUT, v. *poser,* †*mettre, placer*[1]; — on, †*mettre.*

Q.

QUALITY, s. *qualité,* f.

QUARTER, s. (¼) *quart,* m.; three quarters, *trois quarts.*

QUEEN, s. *reine.*

QUICK, adj. *rapide;* (exclam.), *vîte!* — with the invention, (43) *vîte le stratagème.*

QUIT, v. *quitter, abandonner.*

QUITE, adv. *tout-à-fait, entièrement.*

QUIVER, s. *tremblement,* m.

R.

RACE, s. *race,* f., *sang,* m.

RAGE, s. *rage,* f.; in a —, *en rage, enragé.*

RAIN, s. *pluie,* f.

RAISE, v. 1. *élever*[1], †*faire monter;* — oneself, *s'élever;* to — curiosity, *piquer la curiosité;* 2. (to redeem oneself), *se relever;* 3. to — nearer, *se rapprocher de;* 4. they — up for us spirits, (21) *ils évoquent pour nous les esprits.*

RANK, v. † *aller de pair avec qqn.;* to — first, *être, or, se placer au premier rang;* (milit.), to rise from the —, *s'élever des derniers rangs aux premiers.*

RANSOM, s. *rançon,* f.; to buy one's —, (71) *payer*[1] *sa rançon à* (note here that the French say in such cases *to pay,* not *to buy*); also, *se racheter.*

RAPTURE, s. *ravissement, transport,* m.

RARELY, adv. *rarement.*

RASCAL, s. *coquin, scélérat.*

RATHER, adv. *plutôt;* let me —, *laissez-moi plutôt;* I would — die than, *j'aimerais mieux mourir que de.*

REACH, v. *par*†*venir à, arriver à.*

READ, v. †*lire;* to — a heart, *lire dans un cœur.*

READING, s. *lecture,* f.

READY, adj. *prêt, qui n'est pas en défaut;* how —! (32) *quelle présence d'esprit!* or, *comme il est prompt à la riposte!* or, *jamais en défaut;* damn his readiness, *au diable sa présence d'esprit.*

REAL, adj. *réel, vrai;* of — Sevre, *de vrai Sèvres.*

REALITY, s. *réalité,* f.

REALIZATION, s. *réalisation,* f.

REALLY, adv. *réellement, en vérité, sérieusement, au fait.*

REASON, s. *raison,* f.

RECANT, v. *se rétracter.*

RECLINING, adj. *couché.*

RECONCILED, part. *réconcilié avec.*

RECORD, s. *registre,* m., *relation,* f., *'histoire,* f.

RECOVER, v. 1. *recouvrer;* 2.

(oneself) from, *se re†mettre de ;* are you recovered from, *êtes-vous remis de.*

REDEEM, v. *racheter¹.*

REFINEMENT, s. (in manners), *raffinement,* m. ; (in dress), *recherche,* f.

REFLECT, v. 1. *réfléchir ;* 2. to — credit on, †*faire honneur à.*

REFRESH, v. *rafraîchir, restaurer.*

REFUSE, v. *refuser, éconduire.*

REGARD, v. *considérer¹, regarder.*

REIGN, v. *régner.*

REJECT, v. *refuser, rejeter¹.*

REJOICE, v. *se réjouir* (at, *de ;* that, *de ce que*).

RELATION, s. *parent,* m.

RELEASE, s. *délivrance,* f.

RELEASE, v. *dégager¹, délier, relever¹* (from, *de*).

RELENTING, s. *ramollissement,* m.

RELIGIOUSLY, adv. *religieusement.*

RELINQUISH, v. *abandonner.*

REMAIN, v. *rester.*

REMEMBER, v. *se rappeler, se sou†venir de, ne pas oublier ;* death —s not, *la mort ne se souvient pas ;* if I — right, (28) *si je me rappelle bien.*

REMNANT, s. *reste,* m.

REMONSTRATE, v. †*faire des remontrances.*

REMORSE, s. *remords,* m. ; — for falsehood, *remords d'être infidèle.*

RENOUNCE, v. *renoncer¹ à.*

REPAY, v. *récompenser.*

REPENT, v. *se* †*repentir ;* the virtue to —, *la vertu du repentir.*

REPENTANCE, s. *repentir,* m. ; — (for, *pour*).

REPORT, s. *rapport,* m.

REPOSE, v. *reposer, se reposer.*

REPROACH, v. †*faire des reproches à qqn. ;* to — the past, *reprocher à qqn. son passé.*

REPUBLIC, s. *République,* f.

REQUIRE, v. *exiger¹, il faut,* unip. ; it requires some skill, *il faut une certaine habileté ;* he —s a large sum, *il lui faut une forte somme.*

RESEMBLE, v. *ressembler à.*

RESENTMENT, s. *ressentiment,* m.

RESERVED, part. *réservé* (for, *à*), *qui est le partage de.*

RESPECT, v. *respecter.*

RESPECTFULLY, adv. *respectueusement.*

REST, v. *rester, s'arrêter.*

RESTORE, v. *rendre.*

RETAIL, s. *détail,* m. ; wholesale and —, (10) *gros et détail.*

RETINUE, s. *escorte,* f., *cortège,* m., *suite,* f.

RETIRE, v. *se retirer ;* (to bed), *se coucher.*

RETREAT, v. †*battre en retraite.*

RETURN, s. *retour,* m. ; in —, *en retour.*

RETURN, v. 1. *rendre, re†mettre, renvoyer¹ ;* 2. (to come back), *re†venir, retourner.*

REVEAL, v. *révéler¹, dé†couvrir.*

REVENGE, s. *revanche, vengeance,* f.

REVENGEFUL, adj. *qui respire la vengeance ;* — tool, *instrument de vengeance.*

REVENGELESS, *non vengé, sans revanche.*

REVERSE, s. (of fortune), *revers,* m., *de fortune.*

REWARD, v. *récompenser.*

RIBBON, s. *ruban,* m.

RICH, adj. 1. *riche ;* 2. (figur.), *magnifique, délicieux, excellent.*

RID, adj. *débarrassé ;* to get — of, *se débarrasser de.*

RIDDLE, s. *énigme,* f.

RIGHT, s. and adj. *droit,* m. ; — of indulgence from, *droit à l'indulgence de la part de ;* heart —, *cœur droit ;* to the —, *à droite* (*main,* s. f., is understood).

RING, s. *bague,* f., *anneau,* m.

RIPEN, v. *mûrir, avancer¹.*

RISE, v. *se lever¹ ;* (fig.), *s'élever¹ ;* to seek to — out, (71) *chercher à s'élever et à sortir de ;* (in dignity), *s'élever, grandir ;* to — from the ranks, (36) *s'élever des derniers rangs à.*

RISK, v. *risquer.*

RIVAL, adj. *rival.*

ROAR, s. *bruit,* m. ; (of cannon), *grondement, fracas,* m. ; — of battle, *fracas de la bataille.*

ROAST, v. *rôtir.*

ROB, v. *voler, priver de.* (The French say *voler quelque chose à quelqu'un.*)

ROMANCE, s. (novel), *roman,* m. ; (song), *romance,* f.

ROMANTIC, adj. *romanesque.*

ROOF, s. *toit,* m.

ROOM, s. *chambre,* f.

ROOST, v. *se jucher, se percher;* come home to —, *re†venir au perchoir.*

ROSEATE, adj. *couleur de rose.*

ROSY, adj. *rosé, vermeil.*

RUDE, adj. *rude, grossier;* — in speech, *rude en paroles;* — walls, *murs grossiers.*

RUFFIAN, s. *brigand, bandit,* m. ; her menial —s, *ses bandits de domestiques.*

RUGGED, adj. *raboteux, rude;* — floor, *parquet grossier, raboteux.*

RUIN, s. *ruine,* f.

RUMOR, s. *rumeur,* f.

RUN, v. 1. *†courir;* (of a liquid), *s'écouler;* 2. (fig.), so —s the bond, *ainsi est conçu l'engagement, le traité.*

RUSH, v. *se précipiter* (to, *vers*).

RUSTIC, adj. *rustaud, rustre.*

RUTHLESS, adj. *cruel, inhumain, sans entrailles.*

S.

SACRED, adj. *sacré.*

SACRIFICE, v. *sacrifier.*

SACRILEGIOUS, adj. *sacrilége,* m.

SAD, adj. *triste.*

SAGE, s. *sage, philosophe,* m.

SAFE, adj. *sain et sauf; sauf, sauvé;* to be —, *être sauvé, être en sureté;* all is —, *tout est sauvé, tout va bien.*

SAKE (for the — of), *au nom de; pour l'amour de;* for thy —, (17) *pour l'amour de toi;* for my —, *pour l'amour de moi;* for the — of his heart, (34), *en considération de son bon cœur;* and for the — of his cousin, *et pour l'amour de sa cousine.*

SAME, adj. *même.*

SANCTION, v. *sanctionner.*

SAND, s. *sable,* m.; (fig.), *sablier,* m.; my — is wellnigh run, (121) *mon sable est bien près d'être écoulé,* or, *mon sablier est bien près d'être vide.*

SANGUINE, adj. *ardent;* thy most — hopes, (21) *tes plus ardentes espérances.*

SAVE, prep. *sauf, excepté;* — with rare shadows, (37) *sauf quelques ombres fugitives;* —, adv., *excepté que, que, si ce n'est que;* no ambition — to excel, (38) *pas d'autre ambition que celle de surpasser.*

SAVE, v. 1. *sauver;* — somebody from madness, *sauver quelqu'un de la folie;* 2. — up, *épargner, économiser, †mettre de côté.*

SAY, v. *†dire;* did you —, (34) *avez-vous dit; dites-vous;* — (imp.), *dis-moi, dites-moi;* it was said, *on dit que;* as you were saying, (82) *comme vous disiez;* — no more, *pas un mot de plus;* that is to —, *c'est-à-dire.*

SCARCELY, adv. *à peine.*

SCATTER, v. *jeter, disperser, répandre, semer[1];* — (about, *çà et là*).

SCENE, s. *scène,* f.

SCHEDULE, s. *bilan,* m.

SCHOOL, s. *école,* f.; (of young ladies), *pension,* f.

SCOFF, s. *risée,* f.

SCORCH, v. *brûler.*

SCORN, s. 1. *mépris, dédain,* m. ; 2. (object of scorn), *objet du mépris;* he was thy scorn, *il fut l'objet de ton mépris.*

SCORN, v. *dédaigner, mépriser;* she wakes to —, (90) *ses yeux s'ouvrent pour lancer le mépris.*

SCORNFUL, adj. *dédaigneux.*

SCRUPLE, s. *scrupule,* m., *hésitation,* f.

'SDEATH, int. *morbleu! malédiction!*

SEAL, s. *sceau,* m.

SEARCH, s. *recherche,* f.; in — of you, *à votre recherche.*

SEAT, s. *siége,* m.

SEAT, v. *s'†asseoir;* seated, *assis.*

SECOND, num. *second, deuxième.*

SECONDLY, adv. *secondement, deuxièmement.*

SECURE, v. *assurer à qqn.*

SEE, v. 1. †*voir;* gardens are seen, *on voit des jardins;* where I saw ? Pauline, (113) *là où je voyais P.;* 2. *voir, comprendre;* I — it all, *je vois tout, je comprends tout;* — again, *revoir;* 3. to — to the supper, (56) *jeter un coup d'œil au souper.*

SEEK, v. *chercher, rechercher* (à); — to, *chercher à, essayer* [1] *de, s'ingénier à.*

SEEM, v. *sembler,* †*paraître.*

SEIZE, v. *saisir, s'emparer de.*

SELF, *soi;* love has no thought of —, *l'amour ne pense pas à soi, l'amour ne connaît pas l'egoïsme.*

SELFISH, adj. *égoïste.*

SELL, v. *vendre.*

SEND, v. *envoyer* [1]; — for, *envoyer chercher.*

SENSATION, s. *sensation,* f.; to make a —, *faire sensation.*

SENSE, s. *sens, bon sens,* m., *raison,* f.; I was not in my —s, *je n'avais pas ma raison;* in his right —, *dans son bon sens.*

SENSIBLE, adj. *qui a le sentiment de;* being duly — of my own demerit, *ayant due conscience de mon peu de mérite.*

SENTENCE, s. *phrase,* f.

SEPARATE, v. *séparer.*

SERIOUS, adj. *sérieux;* you are not —, *cela n'est pas sérieux, ce que vous dites n'est pas sérieux;* I am —, (21) *je parle sérieusement.*

SERVANT, s. 1. *domestique,* m. f.; *serviteur,* fem. *servante;* 2. (in polite speech), *serviteur;* your —, *votre serviteur.*

SERVE, v. †*servir, être utile à.*

SET, v. *établir, s'établir;* to — up for painter, (6) *s'établir comme peintre, se faire peintre;* — upon, *poser sur;* to — one's foot upon, *poser le pied sur;* to — all right, *arranger, mettre en ordre;* to — the police to work, (42) *mettre la police à l'œuvre,* or, *en campagne.*

SETTLE, v. *régler* [1].

SETTLEMENTS, s. *arrangements;* (marriage), *les dispositions,* or, *stipulations du contrat de mariage;* (49) *les clauses,* f., *les apports,* m.

SEVERE, adj. *sévère;* idiom., how

very —, *que c'est bien riposté! bien touché!*

SEVRE, s. *Sèvres;* real —, *du vrai Sèvres.*

SEX, s. *sexe,* m.

SHADE, s. *ombre,* f.

SHADOW, s. *ombre,* f.

SHALL, is translated in French by the future of the verb. (See Rules, Chapter VI., AUXILIARIES.)

SHAME, s. *honte,* f.; — upon you, *honte sur vous;* for —, *fi donc!*

SHAMELESS, adj. *sans honte, qui n'a pas de honte.*

SHAPE, s. *forme,* f.

SHARE, v. *partager* [1].

SHARP, adj. *aigu, cuisant;* a sharper grief, *un chagrin plus aigu.*

SHE, pron. pers. *elle;* — is a good little girl, *c'est une bonne petite fille.*

SHED, v. *répandre;* — the light, *verser à flots la lumière.*

SHELTER, v. †*mettre à l'abri,* c†*ouvrir, protéger* [1], †*servir d'abri.*

SHEPHERD, s. *berger, -ère.*

SHINE, v. *briller.*

SHIP, s. *bateau, vaisseau,* m.; to take — to, (47) †*prendre le bateau pour.*

SHIVER, v. a. *briser,* †*faire voler en éclats;* v. n. *se briser en morceaux.*

SHOOTING-MATCH, s. *tir,* m., *fête au tir.*

SHOP, s. *boutique,* f.

SHORT, s. *court;* in —, *bref, en un mot, pour finir.*

SHORTLY, adv. *bientôt, en peu de temps.*

SHOT, s. (of gun), *coup,* m.

SHOULD, aux. v. (*should* as an auxiliary is translated in French by putting the next verb in the conditional; when it means *ought,* translate it by the conditional of *devoir, je devrais,* etc., the next verb being put in the Infinitive), your father — engage, *votre père devrait prendre;* nor — any law, *pas plus qu'aucune loi ne devrait;* thou shouldst have few sins, (111) *tu ne devrais avoir à répondre qu'à peu de péchés;* what star should be our home? (39) *quelle étoile devrait être notre demeure?* who — share thy danger, (49) *qui doit partager,* or, *qui devrait par-*

tager ton danger ; that I — live to
see, (66) *que j'aie pu vivre pour
voir ;* if you should chance, *si vous
aviez la chance ;* that thou shouldst
crush me thus, (68) *pour me fouler
ainsi aux pieds ;* that should have
been, (73) *qui aurait dû être.*

SHOULDER, s. *épaule,* f.

SHOUT, s. *cris,* m. pl.

SHOW, s. ; dumb —, *pantomime,* f.,
gestes muets.

SHOW, v. *montrer,* †*faire voir.*

SHRINE, s. *autel,* m.

SHRINK, v. *reculer ;* — from,
se retirer de, être sourd à la voix de.

SHUDDER, v. *frémir, frissonner.*

SHUT, v. *fermer ;* — out from the
world, (37) *fermé au monde.*

SIDE, s. *côté,* m. ; by the — of,
à côté de ; I am by thy —, *je suis à
côté de toi, à tes côtés.*

SIGH, s. *soupir,* m.

SIGH, v. *soupirer.*

SIGHT, s. 1. *vue,* f. ; to know by
—, (8) †*connaître de vue ;* 2. —,
présence, f. ; not in my —, *pas en
ma présence.*

SIGN, s. 1. *signe,* m., *marque,* f. ;
sure —, *signe certain ;* 2. (of an inn),
enseigne, f.

SIGN, v. *signer ;* to — with one's
own name, (14) *signer de son propre
nom.*

SILENT, adj. *silencieux, qui ne dit
mot ;* to be —, *se taire, garder le
silence.*

SILENTLY, adv. *en silence, silen-
cieusement, sans faire de bruit.*

SILVER, s. *argent,* m.

SIN, s. *péché, crime,* m.

SIN, v. *pécher ;* (against, *contre*),
how sinned against thee, (68) *en
quoi ai-je péché contre toi,* or, *en quoi
t'ai-je manqué* (that, *pour que,* subj.).

SINCE, conj. *du moment que, depuis que* (36).

SINCE, prep. *depuis ;* long —,
depuis longtemps.

SING, v. *chanter.*

SINGLE OUT, v. *isoler, choisir,*
†*mettre à part ;* to — a day out of
time, (115) *mettre un jour à part,* or,
choisir un jour entre tous.

SINK, v. *couler bas, sombrer ;*
— down, (fig.) *s'affaisser, défaillir ;*

if this day sinks to the west, *si ce
soleil disparaît à l'occident.*

SIR, s. *monsieur.*

SIT, v. †*s'asseoir.*

SIXTY, num. *soixante.*

SKY, s. *ciel ;* skies, *cieux,* m. p.,
nues, f. p.

SLAP, v. *frapper.*

SLAVE, s. *esclave.*

SLAY, v. *tuer,* †*faire mourir,
égorger.*

SLEEP, s. *sommeil,* m.

SLEEP, v. † *dormir ;* — on it, (19)
dors là-dessus.

SLEEVE, s. *manche,* f.

SLIGHT, s. *manque d'égards.*

SLOTH, s. *paresse,* f.

SMALL, adj. *petit.*

SMILE, s. *sourire,* m.

SMILE, v. *sourire ;* to — on,
sourire à ; to — destruction on brave
hearts (idiom.), †*détruire en souriant, de braves cœurs.*

SNATCH, v. *saisir avidement
arracher* (from, *de*).

SNUFF, s. *prise de tabac,* f. ; to
take —, †*prendre une prise.*

SNUFF-BOX, s. *tabatière ;* diamond
—, (24) *tabatière montée en dia-
mants.*

SO, adv. 1. (bef. adj.), *si, aussi ;*
— very kind, *si bon ;* so illustrious a
race, (35) *(turn a race so illustrious),
une race si illustre ;* 2. (at the beginning of a sentence), (20) *de même,
ainsi ;* so she has me, (2) *ainsi
a-t-elle fait avec moi ;* 3. (bef. the
verb), so ends the record, *c'est ainsi
que finit l'histoire,* or, *ainsi se clôt ;*
it must be —, (49) *il doit en être
ainsi, il faut que cela soit ;* 4. (excl.),
oh so! *ah, comme çà, bien, très-bien ;*
be it so, *soit ;* they stare and wink
so, (59) *comme ils ouvrent de grands
yeux et se font des signes ;* 5. *tellement, si fort ;* who so loved thee,
qui t'aima si fort ; I do love him
so, (64) *je l'aime tant ;* 6. — much,
tant ; who had — much in his head,
(6) *qui avait tant de choses dans sa
tête ;* 7. — that, *afin que, de façon
que, pour que* (subj.) ; 8. so as, *de
façon à.*

SOB, s. *sanglot,* m.

SOB, v. *sangloter.*

SOFT, adj. 1. *doux ;* fem. irreg. *douce ;* the — air, *l'air doux, la douce atmosphère ;* 2. *calme, paisible ;* —, adv., soft, soft, *doucement, bien doucement.*

SOFTEN, v. *adoucir.*

SOLDIER, s. *soldat,* m.

SOLE, adj. *seul, unique ;* — right, *droit exclusif.*

SOLEMN, adj. *solennel.*

SOLEMNLY, adv. *d'un ton* (or, *d'un air*) *solennel.*

SOME, adj. *quelque ;* — lady, *quelque dame ;* some ones, *quelques uns, quelques unes ; certains ;* — day, *quelque jour, un de ces jours.*

SOMETHING, *quelque chose,* m. ; (takes *de* before an adjective), — glorious, *quelque chose de glorieux.*

SON, s. *fils ;* — in-law, *gendre,* m.

SONG, s. *chanson,* f., *chant,* m.

SOON, adv. *bientôt ;* so —, *si tôt ;* sooner, *plutôt ;* no — did he enter Lyons than, *il ne fut pas plutôt dans Lyon que.*

SORCERER, s. *sorcier, -ière.*

SORDID, adj. *sordide.*

SORE, adj. *sensible, malade ;* to be — upon a point, *être sensible sur un point.*

SORROW, s. *peine,* f., *chagrin,* m.

SORROWING, adj. *triste, abîmé dans la douleur.*

SORRY, adj. *fâché de, peiné de.*

SOUL, s. *âme ;* idiom., good —, (8) *l'excellente créature, la bonne pâte de femme.*

SOUP, v. *soupe,* f.

SOUR, adj. *aigre, sur.*

SOUTH, s. *sud,* m.

SPACE, s. *espace,* m., *étendue,* f.

SPARE, v. *épargner.*

SPASM, s. *spasme,* m. ; it is but a passing —, (59) *ce n'est qu'un étourdissement passager.*

SPEAK, v. *parler ;* — to her, *parle-lui ;* I shall hear her —, *je l'entendrai parler ;* to — on, — out, *parler.*

SPEED, v. † *aller vite,* † *faire diligence.*

SPEND, v. 1. *dépenser, répandre ;* 2. *passer ;* to — a day, (1) *passer un jour ;* he has spent his whole life, *il a passé toute sa vie.*

SPENDTHRIFT, s. *prodigue ;* enfant *prodigue.*

SPILL, v. *verser, répandre.*

SPIRIT, *esprit, génie,* m. ; evil —, *mauvais génie ;* spirits of good or evil, *esprits du bien ou du mal, les bons ou les mauvais génies ;* idiom., a spirit of bloom, joy, and freshness, (69) *un air, un souffle de floraison, de joie, de fraîcheur.*

SPITE, s. *dépit,* m. ; in — of, *en dépit de.*

SPLENDOR, s. *splendeur,* f.

SPOIL, v. *gâter.*

SPORT, s. *amusement,* m.

SPOT, s. *lieu, endroit,* m. ; in such a —, *en un pareil lieu.*

SPOTLESS, s. *sans tache, immaculé.*

SPREAD, v. *couvrir ;* a table — for supper, (63) *le couvert mis pour le souper.*

SPRING, s. *printemps,* m.

SPRUNG, p. p. of SPRING, *issu de.*

SPURN, v. *repousser du pied, traiter avec mépris.*

STAGE, s. 1. (theatr.), *scène,* f. ; 2. (halting-place), *étape,* f.

STAIN, s. *tache,* f.

STAIR, s. *escalier ;* staircase, *escalier.*

STAKE (to be at), v. *être en jeu, s'agir, y aller* (the last two unipers.) ; my daughter's happiness is at —, (49) *le bonheur de ma fille est en jeu ; il s'agit* (or, *il y va*) *du bonheur de ma fille.*

STAND, v. *être, être debout ;* I — here, *je suis ici ;* — apart, *se* † *tenir à l'écart ;* he stands upon the verge of, *il est sur le bord de.*

STAR, s. *étoile,* f., *astre,* m. ; — light, *lumière céleste ;* the dear — of thy haunting eyes, (72) *la chère et céleste lumière de tes yeux, qui me hantaient toujours.*

STARE, v. † *ouvrir de grands yeux.*

START, v. *tressaillir ;* — from, *s'élancer* 1 *de.*

STARVE, v. † *mourir de faim.*

STATE, s. *position,* f., *état,* m.

STATION, s. (in society), *rang,* m., *condition,* f.

STAY, s. *séjour.*

STAY, v. *rester, s'arrêter, arrêter ;* stay ! stay ! *arrêtez ! arrêtez !* (30) *un instant !*

STEAD, s. *lieu, place ;* in —, in the —, *au lieu de.*

STEADFAST, adj. *constant, ferme ;* — to thine own ends, *ferme dans la poursuite de ton but, fidèle aux fins que tu poursuis.*

STEAL THROUGH, v. (39) *glisser doucement, se tamiser* (speaking of light).

STEP, s. *pas,* m.

STEP IN, v. *entrer.*

STERN, adj. *sévère, rébarbatif.*

STILL, adj. *tranquille.*

STILL, adv. *encore ;* — more, *encore plus ;* and —, *et pourtant, et néanmoins ;* but —, (35) *pourtant, cependant ;* you have a father —, (101) *il vous reste un père.*

STING, s. *dard, aiguillon,* m., *piqûre, morsure,* f. ; it is the sting of woe that tells us we are men, *c'est la morsure de la souffrance qui nous dit que nous appartenons à l'humanité.*

STING, v. *mordre, piquer.*

STIR, v. *se reveiller.*

STORK, s. *cigogne,* f. ; the king —, *S. M. la reine Cigogne.*

STORMY, adj. *orageux.*

STOOP, v. *se baisser, s'abaisser, descendre de.*

STOP, v. *arrêter.*

STORY, s. 1. (of a house), *étage,* m. ; upper —, (11) *étage supérieur ;* 2. (tale), *conte,* m.

STOUT, adj. *solide, gros ;* (morally), *solide, ferme, résolu, déterminé ;* a — fellow, *un gaillard solide.*

STRANGE, adj. *étrange.*

STRANGER, s. *étranger, -ère ;* to be —s, *être étrangers l'un à l'autre, ne se †connaître plus.*

STRANGLE, v. *étrangler.*

STREET, s. *rue,* f. ; in open —, (20) *en pleine rue.*

STRIKE, v. *frapper ;* (a clock), *sonner ;* the clock —s one, *l'horloge sonne une heure ;* to — across, *traverser.*

STROLLING, adj. *ambulant ;* a — player, *comédien ambulant.*

STRONG, adj. *fort.*

STRUGGLE, s. *lutte,* f., *combat, effort,* m.

STUDY, v. *étudier.*

STYLE, s. 1. *style ;* 2. (manners), *genre,* m.

SUBJECT, s. *sujet,* m.

SUBMIT, v. *se sou†mettre* (to, *à*).

SUCCEED, v. *réussir.*

SUCCESS, s. *succès,* m. ; — to him, *bonne chance à lui.*

SUCH, adj. *tel ;* transpose when *such* is followed by *a, an,* and a noun : ex., in such a hurry (in a such hurry), *avec une telle hâte ;* (before adj.), *aussi, si ;* such sweet words, *des mots si doux ;* and such a prince, (51) *et quel prince ;* 2. such as, *tel que ;* such a tribute as beauty rarely scorns, *un tribut* (or, *un hommage) tel que rarement la beauté le dédaigne ;* with such jewels as the exploring mind, (71) *avec ces joyaux tels qu'un esprit chercheur ;* such attributes as lend, *ces attributs divins qui prêtent ;* such is the new distinction, *tel est le nouveau grade* there is no such name in, *ce nom ne figure pas dans.*

SUDDENLY, *soudainement, tout-à-coup, par une résolution soudaine.*

SUFFER, v. †*souffrir, per†mettre ;* — me to, *permettez-moi de.*

SUFFERING, s. *souffrance,* f. ; her — and his crime, *ses souffrances à elle, et son crime à lui.*

SUIT, s. 1. (of clothes), '*habillement complet ;* two —s of regimentals, *deux habillements complets d'ordonnance ;* 2. (in marriage), *recherche* (f.) *en mariage.*

SUITABLE, adj. *convenable, qui réunit toutes les convenances ;* a lady more — to your pretensions, *une dame plus en rapport avec vos †prétentions.*

SUITOR, adj. *prétendant* (for, *à*).

SUM, s. *somme,* f. ; there is the — twice told, *voici deux fois la somme demandée.*

SUN, s. *soleil,* m.

SUNSET, s. *coucher du soleil,* m.

SUNSHINE, s. *clarté du soleil, lumière,* f.

SUP, v. *souper.*

SUPERB, adj. *superbe.*
SUPERSTITIOUS, adj. *superstitieux.*
SUPPER, s. *souper, m.*
SUPPLIANT, adj. *suppliant;* she is at last my —, *c'est elle enfin qui me supplie.*
SUPPLY, s. *provision,* f., *vivres,* m. plur.; to stop the —, *couper les vivres.*
SUPPLY, v. *fournir,* †*pourvoir.*
SUPPORT, v. *supporter;* (fig.), *sou†tenir.*
SUPPOSE, v. *supposer, imaginer.*
SURE, adj. *sûr, certain;* idiom., I am — I hope so, *pour sûr, c'est mon espoir;* be — that, (50) *assurez-vous que.*
SUSCEPTIBILITY, s. *susceptibilité, sensibilité,* f.; — of feeling, *délicatesse de sentiments.*
SUSPECT, v. *soupçonner, concevoir des soupçons sur,* †*tenir en suspicion;* half —, *soupçonner à demi;* to be —ed, *être soupçonné, être suspect.*
SUSPICIOUS, adj. (in the active sense), *soupçonneux;* (in the passive sense), *suspect;* they are very — of princes, *les princes leur sont très-suspects.*
SWALLOW, v. 1. *avaler;* 2. (engulf), *engloutir;* if the earth could — me, *puisse la terre m'engloutir.*
SWEAR, v. *jurer (de,* inf.); all boys — by him, (60) *tous nos garçons ne jurent que par lui.*
SWEEP, v. away, *balayer¹,* emporter.
SWEET, adj. *doux,* irreg. fem. *douce;* — thought, *douce pensée;* (of flowers), how — they are, *comme elles* (or, *qu'elles) sentent bon!*
SWELL, v. *enfler;* (a heart), *se dilater.*
SWINDLER, s. *escroc,* m.
SWINDLING, s. *escroquerie,* f.
SWIM, v. *nager¹;* (fig.) *tourner;* the earth —s before me, *la terre tourne sous moi.*
SWORD, s. *épée,* f.
SYLLABLE, v. *épeler¹;* — a name, (38) *épeler un nom,* or, more poet., *égrener un nom syllabe par syllabe.*
SYMPTOM, s. *symptôme,* m.

T.

TABLE, s. *table,* f., *guéridon,* m.
TABLET, s. *tablette,* f.
TAKE, v. 1. †*prendre;* to — dinner, (4) *dîner;* to take part with, *prendre le parti de, être du parti de;* to — ship for, *prendre le bateau pour;* to — place, *avoir lieu;* 2. (to seize, to understand), *com†prendre, saisir;* do you — me, *me comprenez-vous?* to — the likeness, *saisir la ressemblance;* 3. — after, *tenir de;* — from, *recevoir de;* to — home, (76) *ramener à la maison, ramener au foyer paternel;* to — to, *s'adonner, s'appliquer, se* †*mettre à;* to — up, *ramasser,* †*prendre.*
TALE, s. *conte,* m., *'histoire,* f., *récit,* m.; — of love, *récit d'amour.*
TALK, v. *causer, parler de, vanter;* if she will but hear thee talk, *si seulement elle t'entendait causer.*
TAMELY, adv. *paisiblement, sans résistance.*
TARRY, v. *tarder;* — long, *tarder beaucoup.*
TASTE, s. *goût,* m.
TAUNT, v. *faire des reproches;* — on, sir, *continuez vos reproches, monsieur.*
TEACH, v. *enseigner, ap†prendre (à).*
TEAR, v. *déchirer, mettre en pièces.*
TEAR, s. *pleurs,* masc. plur. (not used in the singular).
TELL, v. †*dire;* they — me, (45) *je me suis laissé dire;* — me again, *parle-moi encore;* I will not — thee of the throes, (74) *je ne te dirai pas les tortures,* or, *je ne te parlerai pas des tortures.*
TEMPT, v. *tenter;* †*induire en tentation;* that —s us into sin, *qui nous induit en tentation, qui nous fait succomber à la tentation.*
TEMPTATION, s. *tentation,* f.
TEMPTER, s. *tentateur,* f. *-trice.*
TEND, v. 1. *soigner;* 2. †*suivre, accompagner;* 3. *respirer, absorber;* 4. (tendance), — to, *tendre à* (inf.).
TENDER, adj. *tendre, aimant.*
TENDERLY, adv. *tendrement.*

TENDERNESS, s. *tendresse,* f.

TENT, s. *tente,* f.

TERRIFY, v. *terrifier, épouvanter.*

THAN, conj. *que.*

THANK, v. *remercier* (for, *de*); — you, *merci;* — heaven, *grâce au ciel.*

THAT, dem. 1. *ce (cet* bef. vowel or *h* mute), f. *cette, ces,* pl. m. f., are used in connection with a noun; when the noun has been expressed before, but is not repeated, the pron. dem. *celui, celle, ceux, celles,* is to be used; *celui,* etc., correspond to *that one;* if the thing has not been named, but is simply pointed out, use *cela,* and familiarly, *ça;* sometimes *ce* before the verb *être.* Ex., that is to say, *c'est à dire;* that is an expression, *c'est une expression,* or, *voilà une expression;* that would be an excellent girl if, *ce serait une excellente fille si.*

2. — (pron. relative), *qui, que;* the first — offers, (43) *le premier qui se présentera,* or, *le premier venu;* we'd have no friends *that* were not lovers, etc., (38) *nous n'aurions pas d'autres amis que les amants; nous ne lirions pas d'autres livres que les récits d'amour.*

3. — conj. *que, pour que;* (subj.) that he might take, *pour qu'il pût prendre;* 4. (in exclam.), that thou mayest silence, (67) *puisse-tu réduire au silence!* that I were dead! (65) *que ne suis-je mort!* that I should live to see, (66) *que j'aie vécu pour voir!*

THEE, pron. *tu,* subject of a verb expressed; *toi,* regimen to prepositions and subject of a verb understood; *te,* direct or indirect object (dat. and acc. case). See ME.

THEIR, poss. *leur, leurs,* m. f., when preceding the noun; *le leur, les leurs* (theirs), when taken absolutely.

THEN, adv. 1. *alors;* it is —, *c'est alors;* — did I seek, (71) *c'est alors que je cherchai,* or, *je cherchai alors;* 2. *donc, en conséquence;* what —? *quoi donc?* 3. *ensuite* (afterwards).

THERE, adv. *là, y;* there you can

take ship, (47) *là vous pouvez prendre le bateau;* 2. before the verb, *y;* there is something, *il y a quelque chose;* he goes —, *il y va;* there is only one thing to be done, (43) *il n'y a qu'une chose à faire;* is — no hope? *n'y a-t-il pas d'espoir?* 3. when *to be* is followed by a noun, *voici, voilà;* there is my dear son, (11) *voici mon cher fils;* there is my hand, *voici ma main,* or, familiarly, *touchez-là;* there now, *bon, maintenant.*

THEY, pron. as a subject, *ils, elles, eux;* as a direct object, *les,* m. f.

THIEF, s. *voleur, -euse.*

THINE, poss. 1. *ton, ta, tes,* bef. a noun; — adorer, *ton adorateur;* 2. —, *le tien, la tienne, les tiens, les tiennes,* when the noun is understood. I do not see mine, *je ne vois pas le mien;* I am — forever, (97) *je suis à toi, je t'appartiens à jamais,* id.

THING, s. *chose,* f. (*quelque chose,* something, is masculine); love sacrifices all things, *l'amour sacrifie toutes choses,* or, *sacrifie tout;* there is no such — as courage, *cette chose, le courage, n'existe pas.*

THINK, v. 1. *penser, s'imaginer,* †*croire* (see Rules, Chapter IX., MOODS); one would — that, *on croirait à vous entendre;* to — ill of, *penser mal de;* 2. (to devise), *songer*[1] *à, penser à, se rappeler*[1] *que;* he thought of nothing else (83) *c'était là son unique pensée; il ne songeait à rien autre;* she will never think of thee, (13) *elle ne pensera jamais à toi;* — no more on it, *n'y pense plus;* to smile to think how the eloquence of words, (38) *sourire à la pensée que l'éloquence des mots;* to — somebody worthless, †*tenir qqn. pour indigne;* 3. when *to think* has two objects, the indirect object takes in French the prep. *de* (of). Ex., what think you of my plot? (23) *que pensez-vous de mon invention?*

THIRD, num. *troisième.*

THIRTY, num. *trente.*

THIS, dem. *ce, cet, cette, ces;*

celui, celle, ceux, celles, ceci, cela.
(See THAT.) The slight difference
existing between *this* and *that* is
marked in French by the affixes *ci*
and *là* united to the pronoun or
noun by a hyphen ; *ci* refers to near
objects, and *là* to remote objects.
Is this the best room? *est-ce là la
meilleure chambre?* this is some
horrible dream, (68) *c'est quelque
horrible rêve ;* this is his roof, and
he is my husband, *c'est ici sa maison, et il est mon mari ;* this is your
triumph, (56) *voilà votre triomphe ;*
this is her image, (3) *voici son
image ;* this is my bridal home, *voici
la maison nuptiale ;* these are beautiful gardens, (27) *voici de beaux
jardins.*

THORN, s. *épine*, f.

THOROUGH-BRED, adj. *bien élevé,
comme il faut ;* a very — air, *un air
des plus comme il faut.*

THOU, pron. *tu, toi.*

THOUGH, conj. 1. *bien que, quoique* (govern subj.) ; 2. (absolutely),
néanmoins.

THOUGHT, s. *pensée*, f., (poet.),
penser, m.

THREE, num. *trois.*

THRESHOLD, s. *seuil*, m.

THRICE, adv. *trois fois.*

THRIFTY, adj. *économe, ménager.*

THRO', for THROUGH, *pendant ;*
thro' years and silent absence, *pendant des années de silence et d'absence.*

THROUGH, prep. *à travers.*

THROW, v. *jeter¹ ;* — oneself, *se
jeter ;* — aside, *rejeter, jeter de
côté ;* to — oneself from horse,
sauter à bas de cheval.

THUS, adv. *ainsi, de cette façon,
de cette manière ;* (at the beginning
of a sentence), *ainsi, c'est ainsi que.*

THY, poss. *ton, ta, tes.*

TILL, conj. *jusqu'à ce que* (subj.) ;
when preceded by a negation, *avant
que* (subj.), *tant que ;* I will not die
till I am avenged, *je ne mourrai
pas avant que je ne me sois vengé,*
or, *sans m'être vengé.*

TILL, prep. *jusqu'à ;* — death,
jusqu'à la mort, jusqu'à la tombe ;
—then, *jusque là.*

TIME, s. 1. *temps,* m. *'heure,
époque,* f. ; at your — of life, *à votre
âge ;* 2. (repetition of times), *fois,* f. ;
nine times out of ten, (35) *neuf fois
sur dix.*

TITLE, s. *titre,* m. ; — deed,
titre privilégié.

TO, prep. 1. *à ;* 2. (at the house
of), *chez (chez* is used only before
pers. pron. or names of persons) ;
to her home, *chez elle ;* 3. (in order
to), *pour, afin de ;* (inf.), born to
make a great marriage, *née pour faire
un beau mariage ;* 4. (compared
to), *en comparaison de, comparé à ;*
what was the slight to the deep
wrong? (74) *qu'était un manque
d'égards en comparaison de la profonde injustice?*

TOGETHER, adv. *ensemble.*

TOIL, s. *travail pénible,* m., *peine,
fatigue,* f.

TOIL, v. *se donner de la peine,
travailler, suer à la peine ;* I still
—ed on, *je continuai à travailler
avec ardeur.*

TOILSOME, adj. *laborieux, occupé.*

TOMB, s. *tombe,* f.

TONGUE, s. *langue,* f. ; and, by
extension, *bouche, lèvres,* f. ; eloquent —, *bouche éloquente, lèvres
éloquentes.*

TOO, adv. *trop ;* it is — real, *ce
n'est que trop réel ;* it is — dreadful,
(84) *c'est par trop terrible ;* she will
go away, too, in a coach, etc., (49)
*elle s'en ira tout de même dans un
carrosse à six chevaux.*

TOOL, s. *instrument,* m. ; revengeful —, *instrument de vengeance.*

TOPSY-TURVY, adv. *sens dessus
dessous ;* to turn all —, (7) †*mettre
toutes les têtes à l'envers.*

TORCH, s. *torche,* f., *luminaire,* m.

TORMENT, s. *tourment,* m. ; (int.),
— and death! *malédiction!* or, *mort
et damnation.*

TORMENT, v. *tourmenter.*

TORTURE, s. *torture,* f.

TOSS, s. *mouvement de tête en
arrière ;* with such a —, (54) *avec
quel hochement de tête dédaigneux.*

TOSS, v. *jeter¹ ;* idiom., all a toss
up, *par hasard, coup de dé.*

TOUCH, s. *touche*, f. ; one — of human kindness, *l'ombre de tendresse humaine, une ombre d'humanité, la moindre touche d'humanité.*

TOUCH, v. *toucher.*

TOWN, s. *ville*, f.

TRADE, s. *commerce, négoce*, m. ; in —, *dans le commerce.*

TRAITOR, s. *traître ;* fem. irreg. *traîtresse.*

TRAMPLE ON, v. *fouler aux pieds.*

TRANSLATE, v. †*traduire ;* reflect., *se traduire en.*

TRAVELING, s. *action de voyager ;* it is bad — on an empty stomach, (4) *un estomac vide est un mauvais compagnon de voyage ;* — companion, *compagnon de voyage.*

TREACHEROUSLY, adv. *traîtreusement ;* most —, *avec la plus insigne trahison.*

TREAT, v. *traiter, régaler.*

TREMBLE, v. *trembler.*

TRIBUTE, s. *tribut, 'hommage*, m.

TRICE, s. *moment, instant*, m. ; in a trice, (50) *en moins de rien, en un clin d'œil.*

TRICKSTER, s. *fourbe.*

TRIFLE, s. *bagatelle*, f.

TRIFLING, adj. *secondaire, de peu d'importance.*

TRIUMPH, s. *triomphe*, m.; in —, *en triomphe ;* triumph or danger, joy or sorrow, I am by thy side, (52) *triomphe ou danger, joie ou douleur, je suis à tes côtés* (no article is used in a rapid enumeration).

TRIUMPHED OVER, part. *battu sur toute la ligne.*

TROUBLE, v. (oneself), *se* †*mettre en peine.*

TRUANT, s. *vaurien*, m.

TRUE, adj. *vrai, véritable, sincère ;* a — heart, *un cœur vrai, sincère ;* it is as — as, *c'est aussi vrai que ;* (excl.), *en vérité ! vraiment ! vrai ! —* (approbation), *c'est vrai, très-bien ! —* to, *fidèle à ;* 2. *sur, bon, convenable ;* he is the truest fellow in the world, (9) *c'est le gaillard sur lequel on peut le mieux compter.*

TRUNK, s. *malle*, f.

TRUST, v. *espérer*[1], *avoir l'espoir,* se flatter que, avoir confiance en ; — to, *se fier à.*

TRY, v. *essayer*[1], †*mettre à l'épreuve ;* I will try him, *je vais le mettre à l'épreuve.*

TURN, v. 1. *tourner ;* —the brain of, *tourner l'esprit, la cervelle à ;* his head was —ed, *on lui avait tourné la tête ;* it turns their honest heads, *cela tourne leurs braves cervelles ;* 2. *se faire, de*†*venir ;* — conspirator, *se faire,* or, *devenir conspirateur ;* I will — soldier, (16) *je me ferai soldat ;* passion —ed to wrath, *passion devenue rage ;* to turn white with anger, (92) *devenir pâle de colère ;* 3. — down, *descendre ;* — down the lane, *descendez la ruelle ;* — away, *se retourner ;* — from, *se détourner de ;* — to, *se tourner vers,* or, *du côté de.*

TWENTY, num. *vingt* (see HUNDRED).

TWILIGHT, s. *tombée de la nuit,* f., *crépuscule*, m.

TWIN, adj. and s. *jumeau*, fem. irreg. *jumelle.*

TWO, num. *deux.*

TYRANT, s. *tyran*, m.

U.

UGLY, adj. *vilain, tout laid.*

UNARMED, adj. *désarmé, sans armes.*

UNCOMMONLY, adv. *extraordinairement.*

UNCONQUERABLE, adj. *indomptable, invincible.*

UNCOVER, v. *dé*†*couvrir.*

UNDERSTAND, v. *com*†*prendre,* †*savoir ;* to understand fighting, *savoir se battre.*

UNFORTUNATE, adj. *malheureux, infortuné ;* that is —, *c'est n'avoir pas de chance.*

UNFULFILLED, adj. *non rempli, qui n'a pas reçu son accomplissement, sa consécration.*

UNGRATEFUL, adj. *ingrat.*

UNHAPPY, adj. *malheureux.*

UNHEED, v. *ne pas* †*faire attention à.*

UNHOLY, adj. *impie ;* a **marriage**

thus —, (76) *un mariage aussi impie,
aussi peu saint.*

UNHURT, adj. *qui n'est pas blessé,
qui n'a pas de mal.*

UNITE, v. *unir.*

UNIVERSAL, adj. *universel.*

UNKNOWN, adj. and part. *inconnu.*

UNLESS, conj. *à moins que* (the
following verb in the subj. with the
neg. *ne*) ; unless you repent, *à moins
que vous ne vous repentiez.*

UNMARKED, adj. and part. *qui
n'est pas remarqué* (by, *par*).

UNPREPARED, part. *non préparé ;*
I do not come — for violence, (88)
*je ne viens pas sans précaution contre
le cas de violence.*

UNSTAINED, adj. *immaculé, sans
tache.*

UNWORTHY, adj. *indigne (de).*

UPON, prep. *sur ;* adv., upon it,
dessus.

URGE, v. — a claim, *réclamer,
presser une réclamation.*

US, pron. *nous.*

USE, v. *avoir coutume de* (sometimes it suffices to put the next verb
in the Imperfect Indicative without
translating *use*. See Rules, Chapter
VII.). I used to practice it, *j'avais
coutume de le pratiquer,* or, *je le
pratiquais.*

USEFUL, adj. *utile.*

USURER, s. *usurier.*

UTTER, v. *proférer ; exhaler
vers, redire à.*

V.

VAIN, adj. 1. *vain, orgueilleux ;*
2. *sans espoir* (hopeless); vain,
frantic love, *amour insensé, sans
espoir.*

VALE, s. *vallée,* f., *vallon,* m.

VALOR, s. *valeur,* f.

VALUABLE, adj. *qui a de la valeur ;* to be — or worthless, *avoir
ou n'avoir pas de valeur.*

VALUE, v. *estimer, priser.*

VANISH, v. *s'évanouir.*

VARY, v. *varier.*

VAST, adj. *vaste ;* a — deal of,
beaucoup de.

VEIN, s. *veine,* f.

VENTURE, v. *se hasarder à, oser.*

VERGE, s. *bord ;* — of an abyss,
bord d'un abîme ; on the — of bankruptcy, *sur le bord, à la veille de,*
or, *à deux doigts de la banqueroute.*

VERSE, s. *vers,* m.

VERY, adj. *véritable, simple,
même ;* the — boors within, (58) *de
véritables rustres là-dedans ;* the —
sight of a prince, *la simple vue
d'un prince ;* the veriest slave, *le
dernier des esclaves ;* this — day,
(25) *aujourd'hui même ;* that —
hour when, (73) *cette heure même
où ;* to blast in their — blossom
the flowers, *flétrir les fleurs à leur
premier bouton,* or, *dans leur premier épanouissement.*

VERY, adv. *très, bien ;* — different, *bien différent ;* so — kind, (49)
si bon.

VEX, v. *fâcher, contrarier, tourmenter,* †*faire de la peine.*

VICE, s. *vice, défaut,* m.

VICTIM, s. *victime,* f.

VICTORY, s. *victoire,* f.

VILE, adj. *vil.*

VILLAIN, s. *scélérat, coquin, misérable.*

VILLAINOUS, *misérable, vil.*

VINE, s. *vigne,* f. ; wild —, *vigne-
folle, liane, clématite ;* arching —,
*arcades de clématites, de vignes sau-
vages.*

VIRGIN, s. *vierge ;* adj. *virginal.*

VIRTUE, s. *vertu, innocence,* f.

VISIT, s. *visite,* f. ; on a —, *en
visite.*

VOICE, s. *voix,* f.

VOID AND NULL, adj. *nul et de
nul effet ;* to make —, (76) *déclarer
nul et de nul effet.*

VOW, s. *promesse,* f., *serment,* m.

VULGAR, adj. *vulgaire, du vulgaire ;* — eyes and tongues, *les
yeux et les langues du vulgaire.*

VULGARITY, s. *vulgarité, gros-
sièreté,* f.

W.

WAIT, v. *attendre ;* — for, *attendre ;* — on, †*servir, être aux ordres
de ;* I will — on you, *je serai à vos
ordres ;* — on, upon, *se présenter à,
se rendre auprès de.*

G*

WAKE, v. *s'éveiller, se réveiller.*
WAKING, s. *réveil,* m.
WALK, v. *marcher, par†courir, se promener* [1] *;* to — the earth, *fouler la terre;* — apart, *se retirer à l'écart;* — by his side, *marcher à ses côtés.*
WALL, s. *mur,* m., *muraille,* f.; poet., *lambris,* m.; marble —, *lambris de marbre.*
WANDERER, s. *qui erre;* the absent —, *l'absent exilé,* or, *qui erre.*
WANDERING, pr. part. *errant, qui erre.*
WANE, v. *dé†croître;* time —s, *le jour est sur son déclin.*
WANT, v. †*vouloir, désirer, demander.*
WAR, s. *guerre,* f.
WARD (away), *écarter;* to — suspicion, *écarter, conjurer les soupçons.*
WARRANT, v. *garantir.*
WASTE, s. *étendue déserte; les espaces désolés.*
WASTE, v. *gaspiller, perdre.*
WATCH, v. *surveiller;* — closely, *surveiller de près.*
WATCHFIRE, s. *feu du bivouac.*
WATER, s. *eau,* f.; a diamond of the first —, (30) *un diamant de première eau.*
WAVE, v. *agiter;* — hand, *faire signe de la main;* — aside, *faire signe à . . . de s'éloigner.*
WAY, s. 1. *chemin,* m., *voie, route,* f.; to pass that —, (18) *passer par là;* on his — to his chateau, *en route pour son château;* 2. (manner of acting), *course, manière d'agir,* f.; wandering —, *course vagabonde;* it is not the — with the house, (51) *ce n'est pas la manière de faire de la maison;* he has a — with him, *il y a chez lui une manière d'agir;* it is the — with people of quality, (50) *cela se fait ainsi chez les gens de qualité;* by the —, *à propos.*
WE, pron. *nous.*
WEAK, adj. *faible.*
WEAKNESS, s. *faiblesse,* f.
WEALTH, s. *richesse, fortune,* f.
WEALTHY, adj. *riche, fortuné, opulent.*
WEAPON, s. *arme,* f.

WEAR, v. *porter;* to — the shape, *revêtir la forme de.*
WED, v. *épouser, se marier avec* (see MARRY); — to, *marier à.*
WEDDING-DAY, s. *jour de mariage, jour des noces;* — night, (21) *nuit des noces.*
WEEP, v. *pleurer.*
WELCOME, adj. (greeting), *bienvenu;* be —, *soyez le bienvenu ici;* idiom., you are — to your fine clothes, (55) *vos beaux habits sont à votre service,* or, *ne vous gênez pas avec vos beaux habits.*
WELCOME, s. *accueil,* m.; where our welcome will not be, (61) *où l'accueil qu'on nous fera ne sera pas.*
WELL, adv. 1. *bien, eh bien!* — then, *bien, donc;* to be —, *se porter bien, être en bonne santé;* thou art not —, *tu n'es pas en bonne santé* [1] *;* you are not —, *vous avez quelque chose;* to be — to do in the world, (6) *être bien placé dans le monde; être en bonne situation;* to be — off, *être à son aise.*
WERE (see BE); were I, *fussé-je;* that — worse, (43) *cela serait pire.*
WHAT, pron. conj. 1. (that which), *ce qui, ce que, ce dont, ce à quoi,* etc.; I do not know — I say, *je ne sais ce que je dis;* what is past is past, (79) *ce qui est passé est passé, le passé est le passé;* 2. *quel, quelle* (the *a, an,* following, is not translated), — a superb ring! (29) *quelle belle bague!* — a villain! (58) *quel misérable!* — a pity! *quel dommage!* 3. *que;* — a lucky fellow I am! *que je suis un heureux mortel!* — can I say! where turn! *que dire! où aller!* what is this? (64) *qu'est-ce que cela signifie?* — a coward is a man who has lost his honor, *qu'un homme est lâche quand il a perdu l'honneur;* 4. (excl.), *quoi!* (regimen to prepositions), *quoi;* what if we could? *quoi* (or, *que) diriez-vous si nous pouvions?* a what? *un quoi?* what then? *quoi donc?* of —? *de quoi?* what the devil! *que diable!*
WHATEVER (with *to be,* expressed or understood), *quel . . . . . que;*

— his guilt, *quel que soit son crime,*
or, *sa culpabilité.*

WHEEL, s. *roue,* f.

WHEN, conj. *quand, lorsque;*
(*when* expressing futurity requires
the future after it in French), —
thou art happy, (77) *quand tu seras
heureuse.*

WHERE, adv. *où.*

WHEREFORE, conj. *pourquoi,
pour quelle raison.*

WHEREVER, *partout où.*

WHETHER, conj. *si.*

WHICH, pron. (direct object),
que; (reg. to a prep.), *lequel, la-
quelle;* by —, *par lequel;* that
which, *ce que* (see WHAT).

WHILE, conj. *tandis que, pendant
que.*

WHILE, s. *espace de temps,* m.; a
little —, *peu de temps.*

WHILST, conj. *tandis que.*

WHISPERING, adj. and part. (37)
qui murmure.

WHISPERING, s. *chuchotement,*
m.; what is all that —? (31) *qu'ont-
ils là à chuchoter?*

WHITE, adj. *blanc,* fem. irreg.
blanche, pâle; — with anger, *pâle
de colère.*

WHO, conj. pron. *qui, que;* of
whom, *de qui, dont.*

WHOLE, adj. *entier, tout;* the —
night, *toute la nuit, pendant la nuit
entière;* the — universe, *l'univers
entier;* the — of my being, *tout mon
être.*

WHOLESALE, s. *gros,* m., *en gros;*
— and retail, *gros et détail.*

WHOSE (followed by a noun),
dont; whose name he bore, *dont il
porta le nom.*

WHY, conj. and int. *pourquoi;*
— not? *pourquois pas?* —! *bien!
quoi! eh bien! parbleu! why!* (46)
au fait! why, yes, *oui, certainement.*

WIDOW, s. *veuve;* — Melnotte,
la veuve M.

WIFE, s. *femme,* f.

WILD, adj. *égaré, insensé,
étrange;* — dreaming, *qui a de
folles visions;* a — boy, *l'enfant
aux folles visions, aux rêves in-
sensés.*

WILDLY, adv. *avec un air
d'égarement, follement;* to laugh —,

rire d'un rire égaré; so — welcome,
si ardemment, si follement désiré.

WILL, may be rendered in three
different ways in French: 1. as an
auxiliary meaning a simple futurity,
it requires the French verb in the
future; 2. when it means *to be willing* it is translated by †*vouloir;* 3.
when it expresses a proximate future,
corresponding to *to go,* translate it
by †*aller.* Ex., you — be arrested,
vous serez arrêté; I will do what
thou wilt, *je ferai ce que tu voudras;*
I — call them, *je vais les appeler;*
I — go to the magistrates, (48) *je
vais aller trouver les magistrats;* I
— go and bury myself, *je vais aller
m'enterrer.*

WIN, v. †*conquérir, gagner,*
†*vaincre;* to — a name, (16) *se
faire un nom;* — back, re†*conquérir, conquérir à nouveau.*

WIND, s. *vent,* m.

WINDOW, s. *fenêtre, croisée,* f.

WINE, s. *vin,* m.

WING, s. *aile,* f.

WINK, v. †*faire signe de l'œil.*

WINTER, s. '*hiver,* m.

WISE, adj. *sage;* wise judges are
we, *que nous sommes bons juges,* or,
que nous jugeons sainement.

WISH, s. *désir, souhait,* m.

WISH, v. †*vouloir, désirer, souhaiter;* I wish I knew, *je voudrais
bien savoir;* I have the honor to
wish you a very good morning, *j'ai
bien l'honneur de vous souhaiter le
bonjour;* to — joy to somebody,
(52) *féliciter quelqu'un.*

WIT, s. *esprit,* m.; what — he
has, *que d'esprit il a!*

WITH, prep. *avec.* Idiom., there
is with him, *il y a chez lui;* he has
such a proud way — him, *il y a
chez lui tant de fierté.*

WITHHOLD, v. *retirer.*

WITHIN, adv. *à l'intérieur, là
dedans;* — one week from, *huit
jours après, dans la semaine qui
suivra.*

WITHOUT, prep. *sans;* adv.
dehors (theatr.), *du dehors.*

WITNESS, s. *témoin,* m.

WOE, s. *douleur, souffrance,* f.

WOMAN, s. *femme;* — hater, *ennemi des femmes.*

WON, part. *conquis.*

WONDER, s. *merveille,* f., *prodige,* m. ; *choses surprenantes, incroyables; that is no* —, *cela n'a rien de surprenant.*

WONDER, v. *s'étonner* (at, *de ;* that, *que*) ; to — *why,* (38) *s'étonner de ce que, ne pas s'imaginer que.*

WONDERFUL, adj. *prodigieux, extraordinaire.*

WONDERFULLY, WONDROUS-LY, adv. *prodigieusement.*

WOO, v. †*faire la cour à, appeler de ses vœux.*

WOOING, adj. *engageant, qui attire ;* a — *air, un air qui attire.*

WORD, s. *mot,* m., *parole,* f., *terme,* m. ; in other —s, *en d'autres termes ;* word for word, *mot par mot ;* have you no — ? *n'avez-vous pas un seul mot ?* no — against her, *pas un mot contre elle.*

WORK, s. *travail, ouvrage,* m., *œuvre,* f. ; let time do its —, *laissez le temps faire son œuvre.*

WORK, v. *travailler ;* — out, *opérer.*

WORLD, s. *monde, univers,* m. ; she was my —, *elle était le monde pour moi.*

WORM, s. *ver de terre,* m.

WORSE, adj. *pire ;* adv., *pis ;* — than all that, (20) *pis que tout cela.*

WORSHIP, v. *adorer.*

WORST, adv. *pis, le pis.*

WORTH (to be), †*valoir.*

WORTHILY, adv. *dignement.*

WORTHLESS, adj. *qui est sans valeur.*

WORTHY, adj. *digne* (of, *de*).

WOULD (if *would,* as a mere auxiliary, expresses either a condition or futurity, put the French verb in the Conditional or in the Future. If it expresses *a wish,* translate it by †*vouloir*) ; to say that he — be here, *pour dire qu'il sera ici ;* if thou wouldst, *si tu veux ;* as if she would think of, *comme si elle pouvait penser à ;* I — not bear again, *je ne voulais pas reprendre ;* if he — but ask my pardon, *s'il me demandait seulement pardon ;* I — not die, *je ne*

voudrais pas mourir ; and you — have a wife, *et vous voudriez qu'une femme.*

WRETCH, s. *misérable ;* poor —, *pauvre femme* (when speaking of a woman).

WRETCHED, adj. *misérable.*

WRING, v. *serrer fortement ;* — from, †*extraire de, exprimer de, pressurer de.*

WRITE, v. *écrire ;* writing-implements (theatr.), *tout ce qu'il faut pour écrire.*

WRONG, s. *tort,* m., *injustice,* f. ; idiom., let my wrongs make me sacred, (75) *que tes torts envers moi me rendent sacrée ;* — side, *l'envers.*

WRONG, v. †*faire du tort à, léser ; faire injure à, être injuste envers, juger mal qqn.*

WRY, adj. *de travers ;* to make a — face, (55) *faire la grimace.*

Y.

YEA, adv. *oui.*

YEAR, s. *an,* m., *année,* f.

YES, adv. *oui.*

YESTERDAY, adv. *'hier.*

YET, adv. *pourtant, cependant, toutefois, encore ;* yet, hold, *un instant pourtant.*

YIELD BACK, v. *rendre, rétrocéder* [1].

YON, adv. *là bas.*

YOU, pron. pers. *vous.*

YOUNG, adj. *jeune ;* the —, *les jeunes, la jeunesse ;* — lady, *jeune fille ;* — man, *jeune homme.*

YOUR, poss. *votre, vos,* m. f.; yours, *le vôtre, la vôtre, les vôtres, à vous ;* all shall be yours, *tout sera à vous, tout vous appartiendra ;* his home will be yours, *son foyer sera le vôtre ;* these are yours, *ils sont à vous.*

YOUTH, s. *jeunesse,* f.

Z.

ZOUNDS, int. *sapristi ! morbleu !*